They Aren't Just Students

They Aren't Just Students

Making the Connection

DAVID S. BUNN

RESOURCE *Publications* • Eugene, Oregon

THEY AREN'T JUST STUDENTS
Making the Connection

Resource Publications
An Imprint of Wipf and Stock Publishers
199 W. 8th Ave., Suite 3
Eugene, OR 97401

www.wipfandstock.com

PAPERBACK ISBN: 978-1-7252-6205-8
HARDCOVER ISBN: 978-1-7252-6206-5
EBOOK ISBN: 978-1-7252-6207-2

Manufactured in the U.S.A.   04/10/20

This book is dedicated to my loving parents, Dorothy and Rusty Bunn, whose love, support, and guidance have been a constant source of motivation for me.

Contents

Contents

CONTENTS

Preface

TEACHING IS A TREMENDOUS responsibility. Students are on a journey. We influence them during a short span of time between where they were and where they are going. That space of time between those two places is where change occurs. The time they spend with us should be meaningful. It should be powerful. And it should be life changing.

I have been teaching psychology at the college level for twenty-one years. There is more to becoming a teacher than a title. Learning does not take place simply because someone with the title of teacher is standing in the front of the room talking. To teach effectively and truly make a positive difference in the lives of students takes passion and the ability to make a connection. Students learn best from passionate people with whom they feel connected.

This book is based on my own experiences as a teacher. It contains what I have learned in terms of effectively connecting with my students and establishing relationships that facilitate learning via a meaningful experience. Throughout this book you will hear the voice of my students. They are my guide. Everything that I put forward as effective techniques to use in the classroom has been directly validated by them via written feedback, which they've given to me. They tell me directly what works, and equally important, what doesn't.

I make a promise to all my students on the first day of class that if they open their minds to what I present and make their best effort, by the time we part company they will each be a better version of themselves than they were when we met. Here I will make the same promise to you. If you read this book with an open mind and utilize the information within it with passion, you will be a better teacher than you are right now.

Acknowledgments

THERE HAVE BEEN MANY people along the way who have been helpful to me as I endeavored to write this book. First, I want to thank God for blessing me with the gifts to teach, and for putting the right people in my life to make that happen. It was never my intention to become a teacher, but it's brought such meaning to my life that it could not have been an accident. I want to thank my parents for their love and support. I need to specifically thank my mother who suggested that I write a book in the first place. I want to thank my brother Jon, who by his commitment to the security of this great nation first as a Marine, and then as a Federal Agent, has been a constant source of inspiration to me. I want to thank my colleagues Dennis Murray, Bill Van Ornum, Peter del Rosario, Donna Zulch, and Mary Lou Decostered, for their combined support and influence on me throughout my life. And last, I want to thank the thousands of students whom it has been my privilege to teach during the past twenty-one years, especially the "Amazing 51." You know who you are. Allowing me to play even a small role in your life's journey has been a fabulous experience for which I am truly grateful.

Thank you.

Introduction

I HAVE BEEN TEACHING psychology at the college level for the past twenty-one years. When I began my teaching career at age twenty-nine, students would make comments like, "You seem really young to be teaching college." Now at the age of fifty, the comments have evolved to, "Well, you look pretty good Professor Bunn, you know, for a guy your age." I must confess that while I liked the earlier observations better, the latter ones are quite generous from the average college student of traditional age.

That's ok. I've learned to accept this. What choice do I have? Time marches on and with each semester that goes by I am reminded that I get older while the constant coming and going of students keeps them forever young. Someday these young people will share the same perception of age that I do. Not by choice of course, but via the perspective imposed on each of us by time. That is the natural order of things. It was once my job to be younger, and it is now my job to be older. The passing of time and the meaning of life are an existential theme that make up my teaching style, my clinical style, and my personal life style.

During the years that I have been teaching as an adjunct instructor, combined with the years that I have been working full-time as a clinician in the mental health field, I have learned a few things. In fact, I have learned a lot of things. My desire to share what I have learned for the benefit of other teachers in a meaningful way is the purpose of this book.

As clinicians, we gain a significant amount of practical experience, clinical training, and supervision before entering the mental health field professionally. This preparation typically takes place via internships where we have an opportunity to apply what we have learned under close supervision in a controlled environment before obtaining a paid position somewhere. When I began working as a clinician, I was well trained, confident, and ready to start my career.

This was not the case when I obtained my first position as an adjunct instructor. I was well educated and had clinical experience as a therapist, but I had no formal training as a college instructor. I searched but could find no useful book or manual that provided guidance on what to do or how to do it. This was a problem for me. The only guidance I received was a basic outline of what my course outline should look like and include. That was all I was given. Even that left a lot to the imagination.

In the absence of any formal training and without anything to consult, I was equally lost and excited when I started teaching. I struggled. There was a lot of trial and error. Mostly error. Perhaps trial by fire would be a more accurate phrase to describe those early years of teaching. During the process of learning to become an effective instructor, despite having made mistakes, I found there were also things that I did well. Honestly and frequently evaluating my progress is what helped me to become the effective and motivational (my students' words) teacher that I am now.

While I will always consider my teaching style to be work in progress, I have successfully built a clinically sound foundation upon which to work from. An existential foundation. This foundation contains strategies that I have found to be effective in terms of making a connection with my students. The existential foundation of my teaching is solid. This consists of the information that will be covered, the example I will set, and the academic alliance I will build with my students.

The house that I build upon that foundation every semester consists of the manner that I choose to present the information, the way I go about setting an inspirational example, and the mechanisms I will use to create purposeful relationships. The foundation, that is the information I will cover, is solid. But the house is always subject to remodeling. I find I need to remodel the house with each new semester. Sometimes I need to remodel it more than once.

Each new group of students is different, and I need to make the necessary adjustments to ensure that I reach them. Flexibility is always preferable to rigidity. As clinicians we must make the treatment fit the patient, not vice versa. The same rule applies in the classroom. Different students have different needs. We must find out what they are and be as accommodating as possible. And how do we find out what those needs are? Ask.

This book does not need to be read in succession from beginning to end. Each chapter stands alone and is a lesson in and of itself. Additionally, this book is not intended to tell anyone what to do. In fact, I almost decided not to write it at all. But as Rollo May said in his book *The Courage to Create*, "If you do not express your own original ideas, if you do not listen to your own being, you will have betrayed yourself. Also, you will have betrayed our community in failing to make your contribution to the whole."[1]

So, here is my contribution to the whole with no regrets and no apologies. It's the absolute best that I have to offer. I hope you find the clinical examples within it useful, the strategies and suggestions within it beneficial, and the overall content of it enlightening. I am a better teacher for having written this book. Honest self-reflection always leads to self-improvement. It is my hope that you will become a better teacher for having read it. I'm flattered that you are giving it a chance. Thank you.

1. May, *The Courage to Create*, 12–13.

CHAPTER ONE

How It All Began

I WISH THAT I could say that in becoming a teacher I achieved a goal that I had been aspiring to all along. To do so would be acting in bad faith because nothing could be further from the truth. So, while I don't think teaching has to be a "calling" to be done well, I do think it has to be a "passion" to be done well. I am very passionate about it.

I met Donna Zulch when I was a nineteen-year-old, long-haired kid who was playing guitar in a local heavy metal band. She taught the first class of my first semester as a college student. Thirty-one years later I remember that day like it just happened. Donna was, and still is, beautiful, intelligent, and compassionate. As a teacher she had a gentle and charismatic way about her. She was wise yet humble. She related to us students in a way that made me feel very connected with her. From my years in high school I was used to teachers being a bunch of judgmental and arrogant hypocrites whose sole purpose seemed to be making teenagers feel worthless. The Assistant Principal of the high school I attended told me at age sixteen that, "you will never amount to anything." My experience with Donna was a much different and wonderful change of pace for me. Additionally, she worked professionally in the field as a Licensed Clinical Social Worker, so she had a wealth of practical experience which she used effectively to illuminate the course material. My goal when I started college was to become a therapist. This class with Donna, which started my academic career as a college student, validated for me that I was in the right place.

Through the years as I completed my bachelor's and master's degrees, I remained friends with Donna. I began working professionally in the field of human services upon completion of my bachelor's degree, so in addition to being a friend, Donna had also become a professional colleague. On several occasions she would invite myself and other service providers from the community into her classroom to talk about our various professional experiences with her students.

One day I received an unexpected phone call from Donna. She expressed that she was no longer going to be teaching and asked how I would feel about her recommending me to teach one of the courses she had. It was a course named Therapeutic Intervention Skills. This request caught me off guard. I had never thought about teaching. Donna and I had never discussed this before either. I was as flattered as I was shocked at this suggestion.

I asked her, "Why me? I have never taught before. Surely you know other people who are more qualified. What makes you think that I of all people would be good at this?" She simply responded, "When I decided I wasn't going to be teaching anymore, you were the first person who came to mind when I thought about someone to take over this class." I have always held Donna in extremely high regard, so hearing her say that was one of those special moments that I will never forget.

Now, here is what I was secretly thinking inside as I mulled this over. As a young person working in the field of human services, I loved my jobs (I had two), but I was always broke and living paycheck to paycheck. This is not an unusual scenario for people who work in our field. Everyone knows going in that human services delivery is not the place to go if money is your motivation. I also admired Donna so much as a teacher that I was convinced that I could never do the job as well as she did, so I was not sure if I should even try.

Here is what I ultimately decided to do and why. I have always felt strongly that students should get the best experience possible, and the only way I could find out if I could provide that was to try it. I trusted Donna completely and I concluded that she would not have recommended me for this type of position if she didn't think I was capable of it. The other motivating factor was that it paid much better than the other "second" job that I was doing, and at that time, I always needed money. Ultimately, I interviewed for and accepted my first adjunct teaching position in 1998 at the age of twenty-nine. I figured I would try it for a semester and if I didn't like it, or if I was not good at it, I would resign and chalk it up to experience.

And the rest is history. It turned out that I loved it and I was good at it. I have been teaching part-time as an adjunct in the field of psychology in addition to my full-time job as a therapist ever since. Naturally I am a better teacher now than I was twenty-one years ago, just like I am a better clinician now than I was twenty-five years ago. I am a person who is constantly motivated towards self-improvement, so for me this is a natural progression.

In this opening chapter of the book, I want to express my eternal thanks and gratitude to you, Donna. You are a testament to how powerful teachers are. You have been a part of my life for the past thirty-one years as a teacher, mentor, therapist, life coach, and most importantly, a friend. You saw something in me that I did not see within myself. Had it not been for you, I would never have become a teacher, and I would never have written this book. I should mention here that Donna has been my life coach for the past two years, and in that role has served to support and keep me motivated to complete this project. When we found each other, I was nineteen-years old, confused, somewhat lost, and unsure if I had anything of value to offer the world. Your confidence in me helped me to have confidence in myself. I am blessed that you came into my life when you did, and even more so that you have stayed with me through it all. Thank you, Donna.

CHAPTER TWO

To Teach Is to Touch A Life Forever

MY MOTHER GAVE ME a framed version of this expression as a gift twenty-one years ago when I accepted my first position as an adjunct instructor. I keep it on my desk at home and refer to it often. It keeps me humble. It serves as a constant reminder that teachers have an important responsibility that goes beyond simply imparting information. We teachers hold the emotional well-being of our students in our hands. We cannot reach them intellectually until we make them feel safe emotionally. Whether we choose to acknowledge it or not, we are very powerful. The self-esteem, motivation, and success of our students are greatly impacted by our actions, words, and example.

To teach is to touch a life forever. As teachers it is important to be aware that the students whom we have the privilege of teaching will remember us for the rest of their lives. So, the question is not whether our students will remember us, but rather, what will they remember us for? As teachers, we will impact the lives of countless others through the lessons we teach our students. In his book *Staring at the Sun*, Irvin Yalom refers to this as rippling. He says, "rippling refers to the fact that each of us creates, often without our conscious intent of knowledge, a concentric circle of influence that may affect others for years or even generations to come."[1] I once taught basic counseling to a group of

---

1. Yalom, *Staring at the Sun*, 83.

medical students. The goal was to teach them to relate to patients with empathy and compassion. At the end of the semester, a student wrote to me, "Professor Bunn, the lessons you taught us in this class not only impacted us in a positive way but will also impact the lives of all of the patients that we will treat in our careers. I thank you, and our future patients thank you." The ripple effect in action.

The above feedback validates why rippling is a most important concept for we teachers to be mindful of. Statistically, teachers touch more lives during their careers than most others . I will make the argument here that we teachers must be cognizant of this fact and begin to consciously ensure that the ripples that we set into motion have a positive impact on others as opposed to a negative one. The following examples from my own experiences as a student will illuminate this point.

I am currently fifty years old. Forty-three years ago, at the age of seven, when I was in the third grade, a substitute teacher walked up behind me, physically pulled me out of my seat, and screamed at me. When she did this, her face was so close to mine that I could smell the aroma of cigarettes and coffee on her breath. Her eyes were opened so widely that she looked demented. This experience was painful, frightening, and humiliating for me. And the infraction that generated her response? I was talking to the kid sitting next to me. This teacher violated my trust. She violated my physical safety. She hurt my self-esteem. She essentially damaged me. Forty-three years later I can recall this incident like it was yesterday. She touched my life forever in a very negative way. The result? I became very distrustful and formed a very poor opinion of these authority figures we call teachers. A negative ripple.

Another incident occurred three years later when I was in the sixth grade. I remember I did very poorly on an exam. The teacher of that class took great joy in announcing the following, "Well, David, you scored a thirty-seven. It looks like someone is going to fail this class." The teacher said this loudly as he slammed the test on my desk. My classmates found this funny. I didn't see the humor in it then, nor do I now. It was embarrassing, and while the teacher's intention may have been to shame me into trying harder, all it did was add hatred to how frustrated I was already. I failed the class. His methods did not inspire me to succeed. A negative ripple.

And now an example of a positive experience. Several years later as a sophomore in high school, I was required to take a biology class. While I had a strong dislike for biology at the time, and still do, I adored my teacher. She was great. I can still picture her. She was a kind, patient, and compassionate person. She touched my life forever in a very positive way. Why? How did she do this? She was extremely intelligent, but this is not why I remember her. No, I remember her because she was nice to me. She treated me like a human being. She did not care that I wore my hair long, or that I overtly disliked her class. She did not equate my inherent worth as a human being with my physical appearance or academic performance. In Rogerian terms, she treated me with unconditional positive regard. In doing so she restored some of my faith in authority figures, specifically teachers. She helped to repair some of the damage that had been done to me by previous teachers. She gave me what I will call a corrective academic experience. I will remember her fondly for the rest of my life. Kindness and respect are powerful. A positive ripple.

Throughout my career as both a therapist and an adjunct instructor, I am ever mindful of the permanent impact that scenarios like these have. I deliberately ensure that I treat all students and clients with empathy, compassion, and respect. During each semester I request anonymous feedback at various times from students because I want to know what they are thinking and feeling about the class. I will elaborate on this technique in a later chapter. While the comments and concerns vary, there is one theme that remains consistent. Statements like, "I appreciate that you treat us with respect," and, "You are the first teacher I had that considers me an equal," are always there. I am proud of that.

As a teacher, I know that I will touch the lives of my students forever. Since they will remember me for the rest of their lives, I want the memories to be positive. That should be the goal of all teachers. Current teachers pay for the sins of teachers who came before them. Let us be sure to behave in a way that creates positive ripples and does not cause teachers that come after us to pay for our sins. Remember, "They Aren't Just Students."

CHAPTER THREE

"You Seem Awfully Young to Have a Job Like This"

THESE WERE THE VERY first words ever spoken to me by a student, ever. Let me explain why. The first eight years of my teaching career were spent at a local community college. It was a two-year school where people could obtain an associate's degree in various courses of study. It also offered several certificate programs, a nursing program, and was a less expensive place for students to take core courses and then transfer those credits to a more lucrative four-year school. There were many students of a non-traditional age who were there to prepare for a second career, etc. Many of the students on campus were what is considered in the academic world, non-traditional. This means they were older than the average freshman. In some cases, twenty to thirty years older.

This was the case in the first class that I was assigned. I was twenty-nine years old at the time, and I looked much younger. All my students that first semester were at least five years older than me, and several were fifteen to twenty years older. I arrived early and waited for the students to come in. One by one they walked in. I received a variety of looks as they sized me up and sat at their desks. Then it happened. A distinguished gentleman who looked to be around fifty years old walked in, looked at me, and said, "You seem awfully young to have a job like this." He was not smiling, and I was unsure of how to interpret this comment. I wanted to ignore it, but he said it in front of a group, all of whom were now looking as if to say to him, "Thank you. We were all thinking the same thing." I was very uncomfortable. Thankfully, years before this happened my very first supervisor in the field taught me the concept of getting comfortable with being uncomfortable so I could function when things like this happened. That lesson has served me well many times, and this was one of them.

My first inclination was to defend myself. But how? I could not say I had experience teaching because I didn't. This was my first class, ever. I thought about falling back on the old, "I have the appropriate credentials to be here," routine but that didn't seem right either. Obviously, I had the appropriate credential or would not have the job. Pointing that out would have been an exercise in stating the obvious and would have solved nothing. I didn't have any experience teaching, but I had several years of experience as a therapist, so I fell back on what I knew.

My first inclination is always to attempt to hear a person's concerns through, or perhaps I should say despite their words. I thought about the comment and instead of defending myself I chose to go into therapist mode and address what I hypothesized was his concern. He was using a comment about my age to mask his real concern, which was my lack of experience. I instinctively and empathically said, "It sounds like you are concerned about my lack of experience. You are not sure if you will be able to learn from someone who is so much younger than you. Am I right about that?"

Then I waited, and so did everyone else who was watching this. I caught him off guard. He did not know what to say. The rest of the group seemed impressed by how I kept my cool, and how I skillfully put the whole thing back on him. Now he was on the defensive. He started something and had to take responsibility for it. I addressed his concern and then asked him a question that he was not expecting but had to answer. That in and of itself was a good lesson for him. Perhaps he should have thought about the potential consequences of making a statement like that before opening his mouth, but he didn't. He thought for a moment and said, "I'm sorry.

That didn't come out right. But I was a little shocked to see how young you are to be the teacher. As I'm getting older, everyone I deal with seems to be getting younger. I hope I didn't insult you." I smiled and said, "You didn't insult me at all. I appreciate your honesty. I want you to express your concerns as they come up."

Although I admittedly did not appreciate his comment initially, I ended up being grateful for it. It gave me an opportunity to demonstrate my ability in front of the other students in the class who most likely shared his concern. There were no further debates or comments about my age and the class went extremely well. Why was this so effective in winning the faith of the other students? It's quite simple. I was about to teach a psychology class, and before the actual class even started, I had an unsolicited opportunity to put on a clinic in the effectiveness of active listening. The students could see via that one exchange that I could handle a curveball well. They could see that despite my young age, I had the experience and the skill to handle people appropriately without being intimidated or getting defensive. In the field of human services, those skills are highly valued.

This experience was so relevant to me, that I now do this as an active listening exercise in every single one of my classes. Why? Because when reflecting on this it occurred to me that everyone will be the youngest person on the job sometime. That means that everyone may find themselves in the exact same situation that I was in all those years ago, regardless of what field they go into. Because of this, when I cover active listening in my classes, I always start off with this exercise to demonstrate what a powerful tool it is. And every time I do this, the response I get from the student is the same. The student always becomes defensive, and then when I show them how to handle this one circumstance properly, no further questions about why this skill is important are asked.

CHAPTER FOUR

A Semester of Academic Therapy

WHEN A STUDENT ENTERS the classroom, while numerous other problems may be present, there is one overt and definitive problem that needs to be addressed. That problem is how to successfully pass the course. The task of the teacher is just like that of the therapist. The teacher must provide support and motivate the student to succeed. During the process of taking the course, hopefully the student will learn something that improves the quality of his or her life, and experience relief regardless of the grade earned. That is always my goal.

I did not realize during my early years of teaching psychology how similar students and clients really are. As I spent more time working with students in the classroom and interacting with them during office hours, it occurred to me that the wants, needs, expectations, and problems that the two populations share are virtually the same just in a different setting. All the skills I use to connect with and support clients work just as well in the academic setting. Perhaps even better because students are pleasantly surprised at how much they benefit from having the relationship approached in this way. It's academic therapy. Teaching is a therapeutic modality, and the classroom is a therapeutic milieu.

When I had the epiphany that teaching is a therapeutic modality and could be used like one, it changed everything for me. I began approaching this task with a completely different mindset. When I began teaching exclusively from a clinical perspective, my skills and effectiveness as a teacher improved dramatically. My relationship with students became stronger and more meaningful. I began connecting with them on a much deeper level. In effect, I began using psychology to teach psychology. The natural result of this is my students get a much more powerful experience. This is because my students don't simply learn psychology during our time together. Instead they live and experience psychology. Throughout this book I give examples of how this process works by identifying strategies which I call academic factors. These include meaningful writing assignments, real-life case examples, active listening, and the use of clinical supplements to name a few.

Students who are taught from this perspective maintain their enthusiasm for the course throughout the entire semester. The reason is they spend the semester living the principles of psychology and learning how to effectively apply them in their own lives in real time. My students leave each class with a feeling of personal empowerment.

Clients who engage in cognitive behavioral therapy often report feeling a sense of relief by the end of the very first session. This happens because they start learning therapeutic techniques on day one that they can use to begin effectively relieving symptoms. This is the same dynamic that takes place in my class. Every piece of information that is taught in my class is relevant and can be used in the lives of my students immediately if they choose to do so.

My students consistently report via anonymous feedback that one of their favorite things about my class is that I don't waste their time with information they can't use. They enjoy learning information that can be used to improve the quality of their lives immediately. Keep in mind that I achieve this while teaching all the material that is required to be taught in each class. But when you change the way you look at things, the things you look at change. I present the material in a very creative and clinically effective way that captures the interest of the students and helps them see the value of each piece of information as it applies to them in their real-time experience. Teachers often get frustrated when students ask, "Why do I have to learn this? How is this going to be used in real life?" My students never ask that. With each lesson I make it clear how the information can be used in their lives outside of the classroom.

For psychotherapy to work, the client must practice what is learned during the therapy session outside of the therapist's office to see the results. For the quality of the client's life to improve, the client must take an active role in making that happen. This principle applies to students too. I tell my students overtly for the material learned in class to improve the quality of their lives (academic therapy), they must proactively practice what they learn outside of the classroom. That is their responsibility. Those who choose to do this reap the benefits of it, and consistently report how much they like it. The classroom is indeed a therapeutic milieu, and teaching is a therapeutic modality.

CHAPTER FIVE

A Journey of Personal Growth

CARL ROGERS GAVE US the concept of unconditional positive regard as one of the therapeutic factors from his theory of Client Centered Therapy. He thought for personal growth to occur, a person must be accepted without contingencies.[1] I subscribe to this assertion completely. Part of the process of facilitating a meaningful relationship with my students directly involves the use of unconditional positive regard. This can be explained with words, but the real effectiveness comes through in how a teacher overtly treats the students. This cannot be faked. Students are perceptive and they know very well which teachers care about them unconditionally and which ones don't.

Lay people who don't understand how this concept works usually conclude that unconditional positive regard means that all behavior is acceptable and there are no consequences. This is not the case. What the concept means is that the person is accepted while any inappropriate behavior is rejected and systematically changed. This is effective because it demonstrates that consequences can, and should be imposed, while at the same time refraining from hurting the person's self-esteem or inherent worth as a human being.

---

1. Corey, *Theory and Practice*, 206.

It is not unusual for students to think that teachers only accept or respect them if they demonstrate academic prowess. This way of thinking usually has its origin in one of two places. One is the student's parents, who may have shunned/punished the student for not "measuring up." The other possible source of this belief comes from previous teachers who judged the student harshly because of poor academic performance. I mentioned an experience I had with a teacher like that in chapter 1 of this book. I never want my students to feel that way. The following is exactly what I tell my students on the first day of class.

"We are just meeting for the first time, and at this moment I have no idea what kind of student you are, or what your performance in this class will look like. I do want to make it clear that the kind of grades you get have nothing to do with how I feel about you as people. You might feel badly about yourself if you don't do well, but never assume that I feel that way. I would like you to succeed, but my feelings about you are unconditional and I will respect you regardless of how you perform in here."

Providing a safe and non-judgmental environment for my students is very important to me. The use of unconditional positive regard is a key component in terms of doing that. My students consistently report they appreciate the safe and open environment that I create in my classroom. When this is done successfully, students will be more responsive, more comfortable, and more enthusiastic about participating. Ultimately this helps to facilitate the personal growth that is so important for students to experience as they are in the process of self-discovery.

CHAPTER SIX

The Office Hour
The Therapeutic Conversation

THE OFFICE HOUR PROVIDES a unique opportunity to connect with a student one-on-one. I approach the office hour the same way that I approach a typical therapy session. Office hours provide a great opportunity for teachers to demonstrate their counseling skills. Students who are aspiring to be counselors, therapists, etc. will especially appreciate this. It is during these private discussions, too, that teachers have a responsibility to point out and process things that, while difficult, need to be discussed. I will emphasize here that your tone of voice, choice of words, and style of delivery will effectively take these conversations exactly where they need to go. I will give just two brief examples here that will effectively illuminate what I mean.

Here is an example of exactly what I said to a student who made an appointment with me to discuss concerns about his academic standing in the class. "Let's look at your situation together. You just explained that you are committed to passing the class and you are doing everything in your power to succeed. However, you are frequently absent, you didn't prepare for the last exam, and you still owe me a writing assignment that was due last week. It looks like there is a disconnect between your stated goal and your behavior. What do you make of what I just said? Any thoughts about that?" That is an example of a gentle confrontation. The student needed to hear that, but I said it in such a way that instead of arousing a defensive response, it generated a fruitful discussion in which together we put together a plan of action that ultimately motivated him to get his act together and succeed.

Another example. A student made an appointment to talk with me about "another chance" to take an exam. By his own admission he did poorly because he had been out partying with his friends the night before. He was hungover and sick the morning of the exam and tanked it. He made the argument that I should let him take the test over because he could have chosen to skip class that day and requested a make-up exam. Here is what I said. "True, but you also could have chosen to study instead of going to a party. It's unfortunate that you made a decision that wasn't in your best interest. I understand your concern about your grade. It's still early in the semester. You will have an opportunity to improve your grade provided you choose differently next time." This student then made a response that indicated he was annoyed with me. To which I responded, "You seem upset with me, and I am comfortable with that. However, I suspect the person you are really upset with is yourself. By going to that party instead of studying, you settled for less than you were capable of. I know it stings a little, but you will get through it." The meeting ended there. He did step it up and ultimately succeeded.

An important lesson here for teachers is that you must be strong enough to tolerate when a student is angry with you. Much like parents must be strong enough to tolerate when a child is angry with them. And beware the student who tries to make you feel responsible for his/her choices. I used my go-to "responsibility" phrase in this scenario, and I would encourage you to make it part of your repertoire. And that is, "It's unfortunate that you made a decision that wasn't in your best interest." That is a very tactful way of saying to a person, "This was your fault." We all make exceptions for students on occasion, and it will be up to you when to do that. My point here is that the exceptions should never be made strictly because you cannot tolerate a student being unhappy with you. Teaching is not a popularity contest. Students are responsible for the part of the relationship they create. If they make poor choices, they must deal with the consequences of those choices. Be strong enough to empathically teach those lessons. Consequences, while difficult, are in fact therapeutic.

CHAPTER SEVEN

The Therapeutic Lecture
Talk with the Students

IT IS MY THINKING that all interactions with students should have therapeutic value. Since the lecture is the primary mechanism for imparting information to students, making lectures therapeutic is high on my list of priorities. A therapeutic lecture is one that provides not only information but speaks to the students on a personal level such that students leave the class thinking, "This lecture had personal value. It's almost like he was talking directly to me." That thought process is evidence that I have made a connection. When a teacher can generate results like that, trying to get students to pay attention is no longer an issue. The lectures are now therapeutic and the students will listen.

At the beginning of the semester, my first two lectures are powerful but slightly more generic as I am preparing the students for what is to come. I give the first writing assignment on the second day of class, and it is due a week later. Because of the kind of writing assignments that I use, described later in the book, students are inclined to begin relating information about their lives. This is when I can begin customizing lectures. I take course material and relate it in a way I know the students can identify with. And to be clear, I don't violate the trust of the students by using personal information or examples from their papers. That would be wrong. But if I have a class of thirty students and five of them have conveyed having issues with anxiety, I will make it a point to do an informative lecture about anxiety that everyone will learn from, but these five students will take to heart.

I know this lecture style is effective because the students tell me so. The following are just a few of the many comments I have gotten over the years from students regarding this technique. Keep in mind that I never use the phrase, "therapeutic lecture," with my students. I do not make them aware that I am deliberately doing this. These candid remarks are the natural consequence of what I have found to be a highly effective style of lecturing.

"I loved your lecture style. The class material always seemed relevant to my life which made me look forward to your class and want to hear more." And, "The way you related the information is so much more useful than other teachers I've had. I want you to know that I benefitted personally from this class and I wish it didn't have to end." A student expressing the overt desire for the class to go on longer was the best compliment I have ever gotten as a teacher.

This kind of feedback is gratifying. It also validates the effectiveness of approaching a lecture from this perspective. Throughout the entire book I will refer to the importance of soliciting anonymous feedback from the students. Students will tell you when you are on the mark. In consistently getting this kind of feedback from students about my lecture, I highly recommend trying this. The results are fabulous.

CHAPTER EIGHT

The Semester as a Metaphor for Life

ERIKSON'S CONCEPT OF EGO-INTEGRITY vs. despair is the last of his eight psychosocial stages. In its literal sense, this refers to the last stage of life where an older person is reflecting on life and asking him/herself questions like the following. Am I happy with how my life turned out? Do I have regrets? Did I make good choices? Am I content? According to Erikson's theory, if a person is satisfied with the answers to these questions, then a sense of integrity is there. But if the person is not happy, then a sense of despair appears because there are regrets and it's too late to do anything about them.[1] A powerful lesson indeed.

The difficulty in motivating college students to subscribe to this concept is their age. They are too young to truly feel the impact of Erikson's warning. I challenge my students to think about this concept differently to make it relevant to their present lives in real time. I use the academic semester that we are going to share together as a metaphor for this concept, and a metaphor for life.

I explain it this way. "Every task in life has a beginning, a middle, and an ending. This includes an athletic season, a career, and an academic semester." I emphasize the academic semester because that is what I am working with in terms of my relationship

---

1. Corey, *Theory and Practice*, 101.

with them. Comparing the end of the cycle of the semester with the cycle of life gets their attention. I go on to explain that when the semester is over in fifteen weeks, each of them will reflect on their performance in the class, just like an old person reflects on his/her performance in life. At the end of the semester they will each ask themselves questions like, "Did I do the best that I could to succeed in this class? Am I satisfied with my performance? Do I have regrets because I am not happy with my grade and it's too late to do anything about it?"

I demonstrate to students that when you compare the two situations, the questions generated at the end of the semester are like the ones people ponder towards the end of their lives. When I point this out it becomes an "a-ha" moment. A teachable moment. Students get excited when they learn something like this because it's an absolute truth, the knowledge of which will improve the quality of their lives if they let it.

At the end of the lesson, I explain that my purpose in teaching them this is to motivate them to live more consciously and purposefully. If we approach every endeavor of our lives being mindful of how we would like to feel about it when it ends, we will make better choices. By living life from this perspective, while we may naturally feel badly when things we enjoyed doing end, or when people we love die, we will avoid the despair that sets in when we have lived a life in bad faith. We will avoid the despair that takes place when it is too late to change things, and we realize we have not done our best to succeed, not gone after our dreams, not treated the people in our lives appropriately, etc. The final point of this lesson that is difficult for young people to grasp but that they must hear is that there comes a time when it is too late. And since none of us really knows how much time we have, it behooves us to use our time wisely.

CHAPTER NINE

You Cannot Be Your
Student's Therapist

THROUGHOUT THIS BOOK, I talk about how I consider the classroom to be a therapeutic milieu. I assert that students and clients are very much alike and have similar wants and needs. I explain my thinking that learning is a form of academic therapy and how I want time the students spend with me to be therapeutic. But I want to make clear that a clinician in the classroom cannot literally provide psychotherapy for a student. This is unethical and inappropriate for many reasons. Creating a therapeutic environment and assigning tasks that have therapeutic value is not the same thing as providing psychotherapy, so don't do it.

I overtly express to my students on the first day of class that while I think they will find the class to be therapeutic, I cannot take on the role of therapist. I explain this and go on to say the following. "Because I am a therapist, because of the material we are going to cover, and because of the relationship we are going to have, you might think I am a person who would understand an issue you are having. You might think I could help you with a personal problem, and you are probably right. However, it is unethical and inappropriate for me to provide counseling to you. So, if you and I ever find ourselves in a conversation that begins to lean towards your asking me for help with a personal matter that does not pertain to this class, I am going to tactfully remind you that we can't have that kind of relationship, and then I will refer you to the campus counseling center." I have found that being clear about this on day one prevents problems later. Boundaries are important and necessary for safety. Set clear boundaries early and stick to them. Students appreciate this and you will too.

CHAPTER TEN

There Is No Substitute for Experience

MANY YEARS AGO, WHEN I was in college, the instructors whose classes I enjoyed the most, and from whom I learned the most, had two distinct qualities. First, they were great presenters who had personalities that held my attention. And second, they each had a wealth of practical experience in their respective fields which they were able to relate directly to the course material. The combination of personality and experience proved to be highly effective.

I remember taking a course in criminal justice during my first semester in college. It was offered as one of several options that was necessary to fill a core requirement in the social sciences genre. I found none of the choices particularly interesting, so I chose this one with the hope of simply getting through it.

While I was not particularly interested in criminal justice, I approached the class with an open mind. Much to my surprise I found that my level of interest in the course and my enthusiasm for it progressively increased as the semester moved forward. The class went from being one that I begrudgingly took for the sole purpose of satisfying a core requirement, to a class that I looked forward to attending twice per week all semester long.

What caused this change in my perspective? One factor: the instructor. Why? Because he was an actual police officer who worked full-time at a local police department, while teaching part-time as an adjunct. He taught college on a part-time basis because he liked sharing his experiences with students. He felt strongly that knowledge of the criminal justice system was important for people to have regardless of their major or future career goals. He was nothing short of amazing. His first lecture captivated me and from that day forward I was a fan of that class. With his conviction and passion for the course, he convinced me that basic knowledge of the law was not only important, but necessary. He convinced me that I needed this course and that taking it would improve the quality of my life. He was right.

No matter what the topic of the day was, he always had examples from his practical experience as a police officer that made the material come alive. The class became more than a sterile academic exercise that was textbook-driven. All these years later I still remember listening and learning from the stories he would tell. These stories ranged from routine traffic stops that turned violent to the pros and cons of an Order of Protection. He told of what it was like to be shot at during a drug bust, the dangers of domestic violence calls, and how nervous he was when he helped deliver a baby.

Most importantly, as a result of his experience working in law enforcement, he was a credible source of information. When we would ask him questions, he was able to give factual answers. He was able to explain the difference between academically oriented law enforcement and how things happen in real life. He was able to take textbook material and translate it into real-life examples that were educational and interesting. He was able to point out instances where the strictly academic and research-based information was unrealistic or inaccurate. That is a valuable distinction for students to learn, and instructors who don't have practical experience cannot provide that.

I did not change my major to criminal justice as a result of taking the class, but I did learn that practical experience is very powerful in the academic world. There is nothing more educational than learning information from someone who does, or at least did, the job. As a result of this class I gained an increased level of respect for police officers as the front-line workers of the criminal justice system. This would not have happened had I taken this course with someone who had never worked as a police officer, never made an arrest, never confronted violent suspects, and never had to quickly make life-and-death decisions. These are things that cannot be captured in a textbook or be explained by someone who has only read about it.

For the past twenty-five years I have been working as a therapist in the field of human services, and for the past twenty-one years I have been teaching psychology as an adjunct. And like the police officer I described, I strive to make the material in my classes come alive and become relevant to my students. I do this by drawing from my practical clinical experience in the field just like he did. Feedback from my students consistently validates that one of the factors they like best about my classes is my use of real-world examples that illuminate the course material. They enjoy the stories, and this enjoyment serves to maintain their interest and facilitate the learning process.

There is no denying that when a student asks a question it is always effective to be able to respond with answers like, "When I had to deal with that situation, here is what I did, and here is how it turned out." I once had a psychology instructor who was very sharp academically. However, at the time, this person had no practical experience. Anytime a question was asked, the answer started with one of two predictable responses. One, "According to the literature you should," and two, "The research indicates the best course of action is." Eventually I began thinking to myself, "I'm paying a lot of money for this course and I can review the literature myself. Do you not have any practical experience to draw from?" There is no substitute for experience. Please get some.

CHAPTER ELEVEN

The Treatment Plan

THE COURSE SYLLABUS, OR as I refer to it, the treatment plan, is an extremely important document. Ironically, it is often the most overlooked document as well. Years ago, a colleague approached me and inquired as to why I began referring to my course syllabus as a treatment plan. The following is an explanation as to why I began that practice.

I don't want my students to simply learn about psychology, I want them to experience it. For the two-and-a-half hours I have them every week, I want them to live it. From a clinical perspective, the course syllabus represents to a student what a treatment plan represents to a client. I want my students to think clinically while in my class and referring to the syllabus as the treatment plan assists with that. This perspective puts my students in the correct mindset to view their time with me as a clinical endeavor as opposed to a strictly academic one.

There are many similarities between a course syllabus and a treatment plan. Both outline the goals and objectives to be worked on. Both serve as a reference point to keep people on task. Both operationally define the problems to be solved, or in this case, assignments to be completed. Both explain how success and progress will be measured. Both are a reference point to the time frame of the treatment, or in this case, the length of the class. And finally, both point out who is responsible for what, which facilitates accountability. Therefore, this is a highly effective and necessary tool. A thorough understanding of this document lends itself to predictability, and prevents the conflicts that happen when this understanding does not exist, i.e. "You never told us about that," or, "I didn't know that was due today." I end many statements with the phrase, "As per the treatment plan." I occasionally have the students sign a form validating that the treatment plan has been read, understood, and agreed to.

Perception is everything. When you change the way you look at things, the things you look at change. When a student is introduced to this concept and is motivated to change how he/she perceives this document, the meaning of it changes. The syllabus becomes more than a boring, mundane outline that is typically viewed as something that is used by instructors to take up time on the first day of class. It becomes a treatment plan that, if followed correctly, has great therapeutic value and will lead to victory. The solution to the problem at hand, which is how to successfully navigate the course, lies within the treatment plan.

The treatment plan has another function that we instructors must be aware of. It has the potential to generate anxiety within students on the very first day of class. How? Well, contained within every class are those students who have a history of failure and real or perceived weaknesses. The treatment plan can be a vehicle that exploits those. Students who don't write well will fear the writing assignments. Students who are not good test-takers will fear the exams. Students who lack social skills will dread group work. And students who struggle with procrastination will fear the deadlines. These are just a few of the typical problems that emerge for some students almost instantly upon reviewing the treatment plan on day one. After twenty-one years of teaching, I know this happens because I observe it semester after semester.

I have found that most of these fears can be alleviated on the first day of class during my initial lecture and introduction to the course. One of my goals on day one is to instill confidence in my students. I overtly express that I think everyone in the class will succeed despite past failures and current obstacles. I will explain in greater detail what the first day of my classes looks like in a later chapter. But I will express here that some of the comments that I get on a regular basis from my students when I request anonymous feedback are, "Your confidence in my ability to succeed made me feel like I could," and, "You motivated me to believe in myself again." As I stated in chapter 1, teachers are very powerful. When a teacher overtly and passionately expresses that he/she believes in the ability of the students, the students begin to believe in themselves, and then something amazing happens.

CHAPTER TWELVE

The Academic Alliance

WHAT DOES IT MEAN to establish an academic alliance? What is an ally? An ally is a partner. Allies work together to accomplish a common goal. Teachers and students have different roles, but we are on the same team. This is comparable to the relationship that develops between coaches and players. A teacher is a leader whose job is to motivate the students via example to perform at their best and refuse to settle for less than they are capable of. On the first day of class I say the following to my students: "You and I are allies. We are involved in a relationship now that will be solidified via an academic alliance. We have different roles, but we are on the same team, and working towards the common goal of a successful semester. You will succeed despite past failures and current obstacles. I will do my part to help you succeed and you will do yours as well." I say this with conviction to make it stick.

If we teachers do not conduct ourselves appropriately, it becomes easy for students to view us as adversaries. It is not difficult to understand how this happens. Think about it. Students are trying to successfully get through a course, and teachers are constantly placing what could be perceived as obstacles in their way. These obstacles take the form of tests, papers, projects, deadlines, policies, group presentations, etc. And sometimes the attitude alone of the teacher can be an obstacle if the teacher is a negative person. While students are expected to overcome these obstacles to succeed, the way in which they are presented can make a big difference in how they are perceived. For the academic alliance to form and be effective, the teacher must commit to a relationship with the students based on trust, empathy, and mutual respect. An effective teacher demonstrates these qualities through the spoken word, and more importantly via example.

At the end of the first day of class, I pass out index cards to the students and make the following request. "Please write down what you are hoping to learn in this class. What are your expectations? Tell me any topics of interest that you have. This is your class and I will make every effort to meet your needs." That goes on one side of the card. On the other side I ask them to give me feedback about our first meeting. I want to know what they think and feel about what I presented on the first day. Are they excited? Are they nervous? What concerns do they have? This is valuable information for me to have as the semester begins, and it demonstrates to the students that I care about their opinions. I want their input. It puts them in a position to play a role in how the class goes. Collaboration equals success. This feedback is always anonymous so the students can be honest without fear of retribution.

I consider my students and I to be equals. I hold myself to the same standards that I hold them. In the world of academia, much like in the world of parenting, the "do as I say not as I do" approach does not work. For example, I tell my students that I expect them to be on time for class. If students are late, there is a two-point penalty on the next exam. If I am late for any reason, each student will get an extra two points on the next exam. I expect papers to be handed in on time. If a paper is handed in late, there is a five-point penalty for every day it is late. If I hand back papers or exams late, each student gets five extra points on the next exam for every day that I am late. Students appreciate this level of equality and accountability. As teachers we must lead by example. Two years ago, I arrived at school on a morning which I was supposed to hand back exams. The exams were graded but I was in a hurry that morning and forgot to bring them with me. When I explained they would be getting five extra points on the next exam because of this they were obviously thrilled. But more importantly they were impressed that I kept my word. I was annoyed at myself for the oversight, but it gave me an opportunity to demonstrate trust and integrity. At the end of that semester when I solicited for anonymous feedback, many of the students in the class expressed how impressed they were that I gave them the points, along with gratitude for holding myself to the same standards to which I held them.

The academic alliance is a powerful tool. I have been utilizing this approach for years with great effect. Some teachers may be reluctant to try this. They may fear this method gives the students too much control. I disagree. It goes without saying that the teacher is ultimately in control of the class. As a teacher you must use your judgment. If a group of students do not respond to this approach, then as a teacher you must make the necessary adjustments. But I have found that typically when the students feel equal to the teacher and have a voice about how the class is conducted, they behave accordingly. Why? Because the students reciprocate. They show me the same respect that I show them. At the end of a semester just recently a student gave me the following feedback. "Professor Bunn. The academic alliance you spoke of on the first day of class was real. If I didn't experience it, I'm not sure I would have believed it. You treated us with so much respect that it was impossible not to give that same respect back to you. Thank you." As a teacher you can be an ally or an adversary. The choice is yours.

CHAPTER THIRTEEN

The Classroom Is Your Stage

As a teacher, you are a performer. You are on stage all the time. The classroom is your stage so it's in your best interest to become familiar with it. Every semester before classes begin, I made a point of visiting the classroom/s that I have been assigned to teach in. I do this even if I have taught in that room before. So why is this so important? Isn't one classroom the same as another? Absolutely not!

Any seasoned performer will attest to the fact that no two stages are alike. Performing artists always spend some time before an actual performance getting familiar with the stage. A teacher is no different than any other performer. The material is not the same, but the goal is. And that goal is to put on a show that will hold the attention and interest of the audience (the students) for a specific amount of time. The first step to accomplishing this goal is to familiarize yourself with your stage (the classroom).

I begin by noting the size and layout of the room. What kind of desks are there? Is the room conducive to breaking the students up into groups? I explore the front of the room. Are there any obstacles between the students and myself? How much room do I have to maneuver? How well can I see the desks at the back of the room? Where is the media equipment located and does it work? I always check the overhead projector, computer, and DVD player ahead of time to ensure they are functioning properly. Are there enough seats? At the beginning of this past semester I visited a classroom ahead of time to find there were not enough desks in the room for the number of students registered. Solving a simple problem like that ahead of time makes the first day of class that much smoother.

Next, I walk between the rows of desks to determine how much room there is. Can I walk comfortably between the desks without violating the personal space of the students? I like to wander around the room at times when I lecture. While doing this I consider the size of the room and how loudly I will have to speak to ensure being heard by everyone. I also take the time to sit at empty desks at various locations around the room so I can see the front of the room from the perspective of the students. Additionally, I make a note of the potential distractions in the room that I will be competing against for the attention of the students. Where is the clock located? Are there windows which provide a great view of the campus outside? Where is the door located and is there a window in it which will serve as a distraction via activity in the hallway? These are all important details to be aware of.

At the conclusion of this task, I am totally confident to teach in whichever classroom I have just finished exploring. And when I walk into the classroom on the first day of school, I am completely prepared. My stage for the semester feels just like home, and who doesn't like having home field advantage?

CHAPTER FOURTEEN

Motivational Speaking

Having established in the previous chapter that the classroom is the stage upon which a teacher performs, it makes sense to now consider what the performance is going to look like. A student may sit through a lecture despite being bored out of respect for the teacher's position, but a bored student is a distracted student. This drains motivation and interferes with the learning process. It is the responsibility of the teacher to prevent boredom and facilitate interest.

As teachers, we are on stage all the time. A teacher's body language, tone of voice, and affect should convey confidence and enthusiasm. I embrace that concept and it excites me. Capturing the attention of the students, motivating them to want to learn, and convincing them what is being said is worth their time is a teacher's most important task. A teacher needs to realize the attention of the students must be earned and then maintained. This is where being an effective public speaker comes in. Being an effective speaker is not easy and does not come naturally to most people. There are a lucky few to whom public speaking comes easy, but for the rest of us it takes a lot of hard work and practice. So how does one acquire the skills to become an effective public/motivational speaker?

Think about the teachers, presenters, and speakers whom you have enjoyed listening to. Think of the ones who held your attention, delivered a message with conviction, and motivated you to listen. What were their skills? How did they look? What did they wear? How did they project their voices? How did their demeanor, tone of voice and choice of words influence the message and how it was received? What was their body language? How was their affect and facial expressions? Did they make good eye contact and make you feel engaged? Did they talk with you as opposed to at you? What was their personality like? Evaluate these factors and any others that made a difference and incorporate them into your style of presenting. Modelling what you observed to be effective is a great way to improve your presentation style.

I watch other presenters as often as possible. When I see qualities I like, I try to incorporate them into my style of presenting if I can do so without trying to be something I am not. Being genuine is important when attempting to connect with others in a meaningful way. People can tell when you are not being yourself and this damages one's credibility.

I have been influenced by many public speakers. Some are former teachers I've had. Some are speakers I have seen on television, or whom I observed while attending a conference. Occasionally I will see a speaker in a movie who influences me. Sometimes I learn to improve my style of communication just by talking one-on-one with a person. I will often hear a phrase or an effective choice of words that someone uses when explaining something to me that resonates. I always make a mental note of such things and strive to find a way to use them when I am presenting.

Keep in mind that every speaker you observe teaches you something if you are willing to learn. Some provide an example of what you want to incorporate into your presentation style. Others provide a demonstration of qualities that you would not want to use. Watch, listen, learn, and incorporate. If you attend a presentation, look around at other people in the audience. How do they look? Do they appear interested, attentive, enthusiastic? Are they bored, disinterested, and counting down the minutes until this speech is finally over? Which audience member are you? If this person is doing a great job, take notes and hypothesize about why this speaker is so effective. If not, take notes and hypothesize about why and where the speaker lost everyone. That kind of data is valuable.

When choosing speakers to model yourself after, try not to put the emphasis on whether you personally agree with what is being said, but instead focus on the effectiveness of the delivery. An example that comes to mind of a current highly effective and successful motivational speaker is Joel Osteen. One does not have to be a spiritual person to recognize his ability to captivate and entertain a large audience effectively. Watch how he looks at his audience. He walks onto his stage with great confidence. He is organized and prepared. He is articulate, confident, and does not stumble over his words. He periodically refers to notes but speaks mostly from memory which allows him to look directly at his audience members and connect with them. He speaks with them not at them. Each of his sermons has a definitive meaning and purpose. His demeanor puts people at ease. He smiles. He delivers a serious message but uses just enough humor to keep the mood light, and then summarizes with a hopeful message that people can connect with. Mission accomplished. This is just one example of a successful and influential motivational speaker. I suggest emulating successful speakers whose style is like yours. If you are soft spoken, I suggest watching presentations of the late Dr. Wayne Dyer. He was an amazing speaker who was articulate and soft spoken, yet very inspirational. I loved watching him operate. If you are more assertive and forceful, speakers like the late Dr. Martin Luther King Jr. and General Patton may provide useful examples of styles of delivery you may want to try. Don't be afraid to experiment. You will know when you have found your niche because the response of your students will validate it.

It is my thinking that as teachers, it is crucial that we do all we can to keep our audience of students interested and engaged. We must find methods to convey our lecture material in a manner that is meaningful and convincing. It is our responsibility to make this happen. Knowledge alone does not make for an effective and inspirational teacher. How many teachers have you had in your life who you knew were smart and had a lot to offer, but from whom you learned nothing because they did not know how to reach you?

How sad that circumstance is. A potential relationship is lost, and valuable time is wasted. Your method of presentation is just as important as the information you are presenting. We teachers do not automatically gain the attention of our students as the result of our title. We must earn the attention of our students via our ability to deliver a meaningful message in a powerful way.

CHAPTER FIFTEEN

The First Day of Class

FOR ME, THE FIRST day of class when a new semester begins is a thrill, and my enthusiasm is obvious. Meeting the students for the first time to begin what is to be an exciting fifteen-week journey of academic therapy and personal growth is incredibly exciting. My goal on the first day of class is to capture the imagination of the students. I want to spark their curiosity and motivate them to look forward to what is to come.

I begin every task with the end in mind. When I imagine myself at the end of the semester, I fantasize about what I want to accomplish. I then let the image of the finished product drive my behavior to ensure I achieve my goal. In the case of teaching, I have a lot to get through in a short period of time, so to avoid becoming overwhelmed I approach the semester with a "one lecture at a time" mentality.

I use the skills of motivational speaking to capture and maintain the attention of the students. I cannot reach the students and lead them on this journey if I can't maintain their attention. Passion and enthusiasm are contagious. I am passionate and enthusiastic about teaching psychology. Presentation is everything and I spend a lot of time planning what the first day of class will look like.

I typically don't subscribe to the notion that one does not get a second chance to make a first impression. However, there are exceptions. The first day of class is one of them. The first day of class is like a first date. Students size up teachers quickly, so if I don't reel them in on the first day of class, I risk losing them. On the first day of class I come on strong and assertively. I speak with conviction and I deliver a message of hope and victory. My initial motivational speech is impossible to ignore as I deliver a message to students they should be getting from every teacher. Based on the feedback I get, it seems that I am in the minority when it comes to relating to students in this way. I am not just a teacher; I am a motivational teacher. This confident and powerful method of delivery works. The students tell me so.

I leave nothing to chance on the first day of class. Everything is scripted. I choose my words and initial material carefully. I only get one chance to convince the students that choosing to take a psychology class with me is going to change their lives, so I make sure that I am totally prepared and organized. Students appreciate this level of organization because it demonstrates that I care about what I am doing, and more importantly, that I care about them.

On the first day of class, there is specific information that I introduce to the students. It is all clinically relevant, it is all motivational, and it sets the tone for how the rest of the semester is going to look. Now that I have discussed how important planning the initial message is and how I deliver it, I will move into the material that I always cover on day one. Keep in mind that during the past twenty-one years that I have been teaching, there has been a lot of trial and error. My first day of class did not always look this way. The techniques I use to ignite enthusiasm and interest in my students are the result of experience. Following here is an explanation of what the first hour of my relationship with the students entails.

The class mission statement. This is a concept I feel strongly about. A mission statement is important because it keeps the class on task. A class mission statement is a short yet powerful explanation which defines the goal of the class. Once established, everything that takes place in the class must relate back to it in some way. The mission statement for my introduction to psychology class is, "To know self and others better." I refer to it frequently throughout the semester to continuously demonstrate how the course material relates to it.

Students always give excellent feedback about having a mission statement. They make comments like, "After taking this class, I really do know myself and others better. The class mission statement helped me remember the purpose of what we learned." In short, the mission statement is a key factor in providing meaning to the class. And I have found with students that meaning translates into motivation.

The concept of self-efficacy. I define self-efficacy this way: "I will succeed despite past failures and current obstacles." I have the students write this in their notes in first person. I tell my students that I am confident that each of them can succeed in my class despite any past failures they have endured, and despite any current obstacles they are facing. I repeat this phrase frequently throughout the semester. The more students hear it, the more they believe it. This prevents students from allowing their past to define their future. It keeps them from getting into the mindset that past failure means future failure. It is beneficial for students to know the teacher believes in them and their ability. I regularly receive feedback from students like, "Knowing that you believed in me made me believe in myself. Thank you." As I mentioned in an earlier chapter, teachers are powerful. Our words and our opinions are powerful. Use that power wisely to support your students and you will be thrilled with the results.

Inform students of their psychic ability. This is a more intriguing way to introduce the concept of the self-fulfilling prophecy. Here is how I explain this. I say to the students, "You may not know it, but each of you has psychic ability, and it is manifested in your level of expectation. Your level of expectation at the beginning of any endeavor is an accurate predictor of how that endeavor will turn out. If you believe what I said, and you expect to have a positive experience in this class that will improve the quality of your life, that is most likely what is going to happen. On the other hand, if you are not open to what I have told you and are expecting to have a negative experience in this class and that it will be a waste of your time, that is most likely what is going to happen. The interesting part is that neither outcome has much to do with me. Your level of expectation will generate the results. You have all the power and all the responsibility here in terms of what you choose to get out of this class and our time together. I hope you choose to make it worth your while. I will do my part, and you must do yours.

Identify personal goals and objectives. I ask the students to write out what their goal for the semester is. Then I ask them to write out some short-term objectives they will use to achieve the long-term goal. This exercise gets them into the "begin with the end in mind" perspective. I want them to imagine on day one that the semester is over and picture what that looks like. I instruct them to refer back to this goal and the objectives frequently, as this is an example of the commitment they made to themselves and I want them to keep it.

Introduce the concept of "obstacles vs. opportunities." This addresses two things. One, the academic alliance which I explained in an earlier chapter, and two, the anxiety that some students have regarding tests and papers. Here is where I reinforce the notion that perceiving exams and papers as opportunities to demonstrate skill as opposed to obstacles which cause failure, will hopefully alleviate the anxiety that some students experience as a result of academic demands that are placed upon them.

Review the treatment plan. Naturally on the first day of class I do a thorough review of the treatment plan, or course syllabus. Reviewing this document provides an opportunity to have a meaningful conversation. This is where I explain the level of expectation that I have for the students, as well as what they can expect from me. I ensure that students understand the class polices and procedures. This is an important step in forging the academic alliance as well. During this review I clearly explain the meaning and motivation behind everything that will be done in the class, and how it will all relate back to the class mission statement.

Present the "guarantee and the challenge." I boldly say, "I guarantee that if you choose to stay in this class, do what is asked of you, and make your very best effort, when we part company at the end of the semester, you will be a better version of yourself than you are now. My challenge to you is to make the commitment and do your part to make this happen." This always intrigues students as this is not a guarantee that previous teachers have typically made to them. A word of caution here. Do not say this if you don't mean it.

Solicit for anonymous feedback. I always end the first class of the semester by doing this. I give each student a blank index card for this purpose. I want to know what they think about what they just saw and heard. How do they feel about the class? What is their first impression of me? Are they excited, intimidated, nervous? This anonymous communication on day one empowers the students and lets them know that I care about what they think and how they feel. The academic alliance is fueled by the students and I sharing our thoughts and feelings, and I try to get them into the mindset of doing this on the very first day.

Here are some examples of feedback I have gotten from students at the end of day one. "I am excited about the challenge. I think this class is going to require hard work, but it sounds like it will pay off." "I am nervous about this class, but I will try my best." "It's cool that you believe we can succeed. I am not used to hearing teachers say that." "I'm not a psychology major and I didn't want to take this class. I'm here because it was required. But I like what you had to say so hopefully it will be worth it." "This course sounds like it's going to be intense, but I will take you up on your challenge."

So, there is what the first day of class looks like for me. My classes last for seventy-five minutes. With proper planning I can always get through this material and still have time to answer questions and address concerns if/when they come up. During each class, I make sure to give some piece of information that can be used immediately by the student at the present time if the student chooses to do so. This maintains their enthusiasm and motivates them to want to learn more. Patients who see therapists that utilize cognitive behavioral techniques typically report feeling some relief of their symptoms by the end of the first session. I want my students to have the same experience. In my experience as a teacher I have found that if students are learning information that they perceive as only being useful to them many years from now, if at all, they don't maintain their enthusiasm. They get no relief from their academic symptoms. However, my students report that one of the aspects of my class they find most beneficial is that they always learn things that can be applied immediately. Beginning that process on day one makes them want to come back on day two, and so on.

CHAPTER SIXTEEN

Communicate with Students in Writing

I ONCE AUDITED A class with an instructor who clearly had many fine qualities. Among others he was confident, intelligent, and articulate. However, he overtly announced on the first day of class that he would not be communicating with students in writing. He said that if students had questions about their grades, etc., that an appointment should be made to talk in person. Talking in person is certainly valuable, but it is my thinking that written communication between a teacher and student is just as valuable as talking in person. In fact, in some instances I think it's even more valuable.

It is my opinion that to refrain from communicating with students in writing potentially denies the student part of the corrective academic experience they deserve. Written communication is an important factor in terms of facilitating the academic alliance. It is private and much more personal than public discussions. In a traditional therapeutic relationship, the therapist has an opportunity to offer supportive comments, share thoughts, validate feelings, and perhaps offer another perspective. In a classroom setting it is not always possible to do these things because there is an audience and some thoughts/comments cannot be appropriately shared in that forum. Written communication eliminates that problem.

When people have conversations, it is not unusual after some time passes to forget exactly what was said, or in some cases that the conversation happened at all. Written communication is special because it typically validates something while holding the writer permanently accountable for what was said. I always think more carefully when I communicate with a student in writing. My thinking is that the student will read what I wrote several times and may refer back to it on occasion. Therefore, I want to be as clear as possible and choose my words carefully.

When a student takes a risk by sharing something very meaningful within a paper, I always make sure to acknowledge it in writing. If a student shares something in class that I cannot address publicly, I will send an e-mail to acknowledge it. If it is something I can relate to directly, I typically express that along with an experience I had that is similar to what the student expressed. It should be noted here that I am very cautious with information I share and whom I share it with. I never share anything that I think will be detrimental to the student, nor do I share anything that I don't want other people to know. Students are not bound to confidentiality and they do talk.

The following is an example of something that I shared with a student in writing. Doing this gave me an opportunity to acknowledge what she shared in her paper. It also gave me a chance to facilitate a more meaningful academic alliance with her. I will call her Jane, and here is what I wrote. "Jane, thank you very much for sharing this experience with me. While I was sorry to hear about the death of your grandmother, I have much respect for the courageous way that you handled such a difficult loss. I am proud of you. Additionally, I enjoyed reading about the happy memories of her that you shared. One of my grandparents died when I was very young, and reading your story reminded me of some happy memories of her that I had not thought of in a long time. It was helpful to me. Thank you."

Later in the day after giving the paper back to her, I received the following e-mail. "Professor Bunn, when I read the comments you made on my paper I nearly cried. You are the first person in my life to ever express being proud of me for anything. And to know that something I said was helpful to you made me feel special. Thanks Professor Bunn."

This student shared with me in a previous paper that she had been raised in a very punitive environment, absent of love and support. The comments that I shared with her in writing turned out to be powerful and therapeutic. Had I not taken the time to share my thoughts with her, this meaningful exchange would never have happened. Exchanges like these solidify the academic alliance and facilitate a corrective academic experience.

Written communication is important and provides teachers with an opportunity to connect with students in a meaningful and appropriate way. This was just one of countless examples of how I utilize written communication to acknowledge the efforts of my students while at the same time supporting the academic alliance.

CHAPTER SEVENTEEN

Show Random Acts of Kindness

KINDNESS COUNTS. NO MATTER what subject you teach, adding a touch of humanity to it will only make it better. Remember, they aren't just students. They are human beings with thoughts, feelings, problems, and lives. To reach them intellectually you must connect with them emotionally. Phrases like, "little things mean a lot," and "it's the thought that counts," are relevant in every relationship if it is to be meaningful. The more deposits you make in the "relationship bank account," the stronger the bond will be. Teachers must capitalize on opportunities to be kind as they come up. And these opportunities are always there if you look for them. The following is an example.

A few years ago, a student in one of my classes experienced the tragic and unexpected death of a close family friend. This event took place shortly before the semester was to end. The memorial services were going to directly interfere with his ability to be present for a major exam. When he approached me with this dilemma, he was visibly shaken and understandably upset. My immediate response was, "I am so sorry for your loss. Please do whatever is necessary to take care of yourself. We can reschedule the exam." I demonstrated empathy and compassion, as I hope any teacher would. He was grateful for my being flexible with the exam date.

He made up the exam before the semester was over and moved on as planned.

Six weeks later after the new semester began, I was wondering how he was doing and decided to send him an e-mail. It read, "Hello. You had a very difficult experience towards the end of last semester. I just wanted to check in and see how you are doing. I hope the new semester is going well for you." This was just a simple message that took only a moment of my time to write, but it proved to be very meaningful to him. He wrote back, "Hey Professor Bunn, thank you so much for your e-mail. That was very thoughtful. You are the only one of my professors who thought to check in with me since that happened. My semester is going fine, and I hope yours is too. Thanks."

Most recently I taught a class of graduate level students who were about to be observed while conducting standardized patient interviews. I was aware of this, and part of my task in this class was to help them learn the necessary skills to conduct such interviews. The students typically congregated every evening in a specific classroom to study together. I stopped by the classroom on my way home that night to check in and hear about how their interviews went. The students appreciated my concern and were flattered that I went out of my way to check on them. Once again, this only took a few moments of my time, but it was very meaningful to them. They were grateful that I let them matter to me and that I was invested in their success. One of them mentioned this specifically in the final reflection paper.

These are just a few examples of how random acts of kindness are so powerful. If you want your students to know they matter to you, then you must show them they matter to you. Random acts of kindness are free to give, but the dividends are priceless. Students will remember us for the rest of our lives. What have you done to ensure that your students will remember you for something nice?

CHAPTER EIGHTEEN

Tell Your Story If You Have One

WHEN I WAS THIRTEEN years old, I experienced my first major depressive episode. My world suddenly and without warning became a dark and frightening place. I became socially withdrawn and extremely unhappy. I pulled away from friends, stopped practicing the guitar, no longer cared about baseball, and began doing poorly in school. Despite these factors, I was spared suicidal ideation. In fact, death anxiety turned out to be a large part of the problem and would continue to be a powerful theme throughout my life.

While this did not literally happen overnight, it did set in quickly. There was a sharp decline in all areas of my functioning. It soon became clear that this was a problem that I was not going to be able to think my way out of or simply get over. Fortunately, my parents realized this, and they connected me with my first therapist. He was great. I saw him weekly for nearly a year. Within the first few months my symptoms decreased, and I began feeling better. Eventually my life went pretty much back to normal, and to me this was nothing short of amazing. To this day I credit that therapist with saving my life.

As a result of that experience, I was exposed to two things that changed my life forever. One, I experienced first hand how devastating and painful a mental health issue can be. I learned how much suffering it can cause and saw the impact it had not only on how I viewed myself, but how other people viewed and treated me. Two, I discovered the miracle of psychotherapy. That therapist saved my life. At the time I did not know how or why talking to this person every week helped me. I just knew that it did. At the time that was good enough for me. It was because of him and that experience that I decided to become a therapist myself. Now in retrospect I understand how and why this therapist helped me. It wasn't his theoretical approach that made the impact, it was his compassion and understanding that really helped me connect with him and make a recovery.

My story, while unique to me, is not unusual at all. Perhaps my willingness to share it openly is. The mental health field is full of practitioners better known as "wounded healers." These are people, who much like me, have experienced some personal trauma, survived it, and in turn became motivated to help others survive too. Altruism is a wonderful gift and therapeutic in and of itself.

Now, thirty-seven years later, I still experience depressive episodes on occasion. At this point in my life I don't fear them. I have learned to cope with my own depression when it comes to visit, and I know it will pass. History has validated that. When I was younger, I was angry that I developed this problem, but now I am thankful for it. I have learned that for me a depressive episode is not simply an inconvenience. There is typically a meaning for it. Usually it is because I am not handling something in my life correctly. Perhaps I am denying some problem that needs to be addressed, or maybe I am being incongruent such that my behavior is not in-line with my values. Despite the reason, I can usually pinpoint what needs to be addressed and then I make the appropriate adjustments.

Having a mental health issue of my own has helped me in terms of my ability to empathize with people who are having problems. While the root of another person's suffering may be different than mine, I understand what it feels like to suffer. Being familiar with that feeling allows me to effectively connect with others who are suffering. When a person I am working with gets a sense of that, a connection is made, and the healing process can begin. Through my experience with depression I have learned that there is meaning and personal growth to be found through suffering. I have also learned that happiness and the constant pursuit of it is greatly overrated.

I share this story with my students very early in the relationship while I am in the process of establishing the academic alliance. I do this for three reasons. One, I want to establish credibility with my students and connect with them. I know that every semester there are students in my classes who are dealing with a mental illness of some kind. Telling them my story gives them hope and helps them feel less isolated. Two, it allows my students to see that having a mental health issue does not have to destroy one's life, dictate the quality of it, or define who one is. And three, my willingness to share things about myself with them motivates them to share things about themselves with me. I want to know what my students are dealing with. By sharing my story candidly, I create a safe environment for them to share their stories with me, and they do.

Relationships are driven by human experience. When students feel comfortable sharing intimate and emotionally charged details of their lives, their experience in the class becomes more meaningful. This kind of sharing facilitates a deeper connection. Students who share their stories assist each other via altruism, and by doing so help others who may be experiencing similar problems to feel less isolated. Everybody wins.

There is a clinically driven reason for everything that I do, say, and assign in my classes. This kind of sharing reinforces that the classroom is in fact a therapeutic milieu. It creates an environment where healing takes place via education. Share your story if you have one. The therapeutic value will be wonderful.

CHAPTER NINETEEN

Sharing Facilitates Intimacy

IN THE EARLY 90S, famous musician Eric Clapton suffered a terrible loss. His four-year-old son in a tragic accident fell from an apartment window to his death. Eric was devastated. He fell into such a depressed state that people who were close to him reportedly feared for his safety. Eric's close friend and equally famous musician Phil Collins said that Eric was grieving so hard that there was concern that he might take his own life.

As a result of this situation, Eric Clapton went on to write one of his biggest hits. It was a song called "Tears in Heaven." Writing the song was therapeutic for Eric and helped him cope with the loss. In an interview, Eric was asked about his motivation for writing the song. I was deeply moved by his response and have never forgotten it. I am paraphrasing here, but what he basically said was this. "I have an intimate relationship with my fans. They knew I was in pain. I thought it would be wrong to for me to try and hide this and not allow them to experience it with me. Writing this song allowed me to share my grief with my fans. It brought us closer together."

Eric Clapton has millions of fans. I am one of them. And like most of his other fans, I will never get to meet him, yet he said that he has an intimate relationship with us. I would agree, but how is this possible? The reason is because he relates to us in a genuine way. He has other songs in which he shares emotional experiences from his life with us too. For example, in the song "Layla" he tells us about the turbulent relationship he once had with the ex-wife of former Beatle George Harrison. He has another song called "Wonderful Tonight" where he shares with us the details of a romantic evening he and his wife had. Through his music Eric shows us his humanity. He has allowed us to share his ups and downs. He has not been afraid to let us see him when he was most vulnerable. His willingness to do this has forged the intimate relationship that he has with we, his fans.

As a teacher, this is the kind of relationship that I strive to establish with my students. I don't want them to view me as just another teacher whose class they have to pass in order to achieve some future goal. I want them to see my humanity. I want them to see me as a fellow human being who, like them, is doing the best that he can to make the most out of life. I want them to realize that I have the same ups and downs that they do, and that the world has and will continue to treat me in the same wonderful and sometimes cruel way that it does everyone else. I share appropriate details of my life with my students regularly throughout the semester to establish a genuine and meaningful relationship with them. Once again, I will remind the reader that you should be cautious and use your judgment when making disclosures. You should never disclose anything that could be harmful to the students, and you should not disclose anything that you don't want other people to know. Students are not bound to confidentiality and they do talk.

Here is an example of something that I shared with my students as I attempted to be genuine with them. My father died a week after Thanksgiving one fall semester. He had been in poor health for most of the previous year so while his death was not a shock, it was nonetheless very painful. We were close and I've had difficulty coping with the loss. His death took place when I was scheduled to review material with my students for the final exam. The wake and funeral services were not in conflict with my teaching schedule, so I decided not to cancel my classes. My father was a professional fire fighter. He was a hero who always put the needs of other people before his own. I was sure that he would not have wanted me to cancel my classes and deprive my students of having a review session which they were counting on. The following is exactly what I said to them.

"Good morning everyone. Before we get started today, there is something that I want to share with you. Two days ago, my father died. The memorial services did not conflict with our class, so I decided not to cancel it. My father was a fire fighter who always put the needs of others ahead of his own, and I know he would not have wanted me to cancel our review session today. Additionally, I know how important it is to you that we review before the final exam, so I didn't want to deprive you of that. However, I must admit that I am in pain right now. I know that I will appear distant today and not quite myself, and this is the reason why. My current mood has nothing to do with you or my feelings about being here. I could have attempted to conceal this from you, but we are in a relationship and I thought it was better to tell you the truth. Having said that, let's begin our review."

My choice to share this information with my students was the right one, and it generated valuable results. It gave me an opportunity to demonstrate being genuine. In knew I looked "off" that day, and that my students would pick up on it. Rather than make them wonder why, I thought it was best to tell them. It gave me an opportunity to honor my father and share some of him with them. It also allowed me to demonstrate that it is possible to be in pain and still follow through on one's responsibilities. And finally, it brought us closer together. Many students reached out to me via e-mail that day. Some did this to respectfully express their condolences. Some of them shared their understanding of my grief because they too had experienced the death of a parent. And others simply thanked me for respecting them enough to tell them about this. By sharing this experience with my students, I allowed my father to continue to fulfill what he thought was his mission in life, which was to help people, and like Eric Clapton, I allowed the students to experience my grief with me.

CHAPTER TWENTY

Eighteen and Life

Experience That Is

IF SOMEONE EXPRESSES HAVING eighteen years of experience working at the same job, or playing an instrument, or practicing yoga, we are inclined to conclude the person possesses a high degree of wisdom or talent. Surely after having invested that much time in something this person must be an authority. We generally take this on faith regardless of whether the person has overtly demonstrated anything besides lip service.

The problem I grapple with is how come eighteen years of experience is considered long enough to be an expert at anything, except life. The average eighteen-year-old is not typically considered by older adults to be wise or experienced. Older adults tend to dismiss these younger people. We say things like, "She is only eighteen. What could she possibly know?" Or we might say, "He is only eighteen, he has no idea how tough life can be." We don't endow an eighteen-year-old as wise or mature. But ironically, we allow them to go to war and we expect them to have an idea about what they want to do with their lives before they even leave high school.

During the years that I have been teaching college, the average age of my students has been eighteen. With my combined experience of doing clinical work with adolescents and being a college teacher, I can say with confidence and credibility that a lot can happen to a person between birth and age eighteen. I have found that my eighteen-year-old students have gotten a wealth of wisdom and experience from the challenges that life has already presented them with. I make a point of honoring that wisdom as much as possible. Through the safe classroom environment that I create and the writing assignments I give, students are encouraged to talk and write about their life experiences. I want them to share those with me. Some of the most profound lessons I have learned have come from these young people who are less than half my age. The following are just some of the life experiences that my eighteen-year-old students have shared with me over the years.

Divorce. Death of parents. Personal addiction. Parent with an addiction. Domestic violence. Loss of someone to suicide. Eating disorder. Mental illness. Loss of friend to terrorist violence in another country. Death of a sibling. Serious physical illness. Victim of bullying. Cheated on by a partner. Sexually transmitted disease. Loss of home to a fire. Disabled from an accident. Victim of a hate crime. Survivor of drug overdose. Poverty. Failing out of a previous school. PTSD. Loss of a loved one in a foreign war. And the list goes on.

Look at this list and then tell me that a person who is "only" eighteen years old does not know anything. Tell me someone who is "only" eighteen years old doesn't have life experience or know what it means to suffer. I dare say that many of the eighteen-year-old people that I've had the privilege to work with and learn from over the years have more wisdom and life experience than many older people I know.

In my classes I overtly demonstrate honor and respect for my students and the variety of experiences they've already endured in their short lives. I acknowledge how strong and brave they are. I assist them through class discussions, therapeutic lectures, and writing assignments to evaluate their experiences and use what they have learned from their pasts. I encourage them to use what they have learned to become better versions of themselves as life continues to present them with new challenges. Students appreciate this. They find this validating.

One thing I've learned for sure is this. While some older people are wise, wisdom does not come automatically with age. Wisdom comes from experience, period. My students and yours have an abundance of it. I would encourage you to tap into it.

CHAPTER TWENTY-ONE

What Do You Think I Should Do?

ONE OF THE MOST important tasks that we teachers have is to teach students how to make decisions and take responsibility for them. All therapists know that giving people advice or, worse yet, making decisions for them is inappropriate. Doing this weakens people and deprives them of the opportunity to grow.

Consider the drawbacks to giving advice to students. If the advice is taken and it works out, the student cannot take responsibility for it because the credit for the success must go to the teacher. If the advice is taken and it doesn't work out, the teacher runs the risk of being blamed for whatever catastrophe ensues as the result, and the student does not have to take responsibility for that either. Yes, the business of giving advice is a risky one that teachers and therapists should avoid.

If this is the case, then why do so many people in these positions give advice? There could be any number of reasons, but I will limit this list to the ones that I am directly aware of. Some teachers feel the need to be needed. This harms the student by encouraging dependency. In this case the teacher is getting his/her own needs met as opposed to considering what is best for the student. Lack of patience. This advice-giver needs the problem to be solved immediately. And finally, the inability to tolerate letting someone struggle a little. Learning to make decisions and take responsibility for them can be difficult and painful but sparing students of this hinders their growth and development.

When a student approaches me and says, "Professor Bunn, what do you think I should do?" I have found it best to do the following. I assist the student with identifying the possible solutions to the dilemma along with the potential consequence of each choice. Upon doing that, the student is on his/her own. Despite all my years as a teacher and a therapist, I am still of the mindset that I don't truly know what is best for someone, so I proceed in this fashion and let the student struggle. They are not always happy with my approach, but I am strong enough to tolerate that. Because of the relationship that I establish with my students, they know I have their best interest in mind. The following is a snapshot of a conversation that I had with a student years ago who began the discussion with, "What do you think I should do?" The student was struggling in the course and was trying to decide whether to drop it before the deadline. Here is what I ultimately said.

"You have a tough decision to make, and you would like me to make it for you, to tell you what you should do. The fact is I don't know. We've discussed the changes in your study habits that need to happen and the grades you need to get to be successful. The add/drop deadline is three days away. Take some time and think it over. You are an adult and I am confident you will make the decision that is in your best interest."

The following week I received an e-mail from the college letting me know this student had dropped the course. Truth be told, this is not what I had hoped for. In my opinion this student had the ability to make the necessary changes to be successful. But that was *my opinion*. Had I told him that he may have decided to stay and run the risk of failing. Instead of offering my opinion, I assured him of being capable of making the choice that was right for him on his own, and that is what he did. He made a decision and took responsibility for it. Never give advice.

CHAPTER TWENTY-TWO

When the Best of Intentions Went Wrong

As a teacher, one of the primary issues that I see students struggle with on a regular basis is test anxiety. This is one of the reasons why during my initial lecture on the first day of class I urge students to look at exams as opportunities as opposed to obstacles. My goal here is to assist students who have test anxiety to perceive exams in a more positive way. Students who have test anxiety put themselves at a disadvantage. Students with this problem often say to me, "I studied for hours and I was confident that I knew everything, but when you put the test in front of me, I got so nervous that I forgot what I knew." That is the usual theme.

One morning when I was about to give an exam, I attempted to alleviate the test anxiety that some of my students had by giving them a pep talk before I handed it out. I reminded them that we did a thorough review in class to ensure they were aware of the material that was going to be on the exam. Then I said, "And this is without question the easiest exam that I have ever given." I thought that upon hearing that, the anxiety would decrease. This may have worked for some, but not for everyone.

Later that day I received an e-mail from a student that said, "Professor Bunn, I know you said that today's exam was the easiest one you ever gave. I just wanted to tell you before you grade mine how badly I feel that I tanked it. I always feel bad when I screw up a test, but I feel even worse about this one because you said it was supposed to be easy. I'm sorry about that. I really did do my best."

Naturally I felt terrible. When I announced to the class that this was the easiest exam I had ever given, I only considered the positive effect I was going for. I did not stop and think about the negative impact this announcement could have on students who might not do well. This student's e-mail made me painfully aware that this statement, which I made with the best of intentions, had the potential to do damage. Upon reading that e-mail I thought to myself, "Of course a student is going to feel worse if you tell him that an exam is the easiest one ever and he does poorly. How could I have not considered that possibility?" One of the many things I have learned about myself over the years is that sometimes I get so excited about thinking I have solved a problem that I don't always consider what could happen if the intervention were to go wrong. Lesson learned.

I wrote back to this student and apologized for how I had inadvertently made him feel bad. It would have been easier to tell him the test was just as difficult as any other that I had given and that I said it was easy to help people relax. I chose not to do this because I would have been lying and thus acting in bad faith. Why? Because the fact is, it was the easiest exam I had ever given (in my opinion). He knew I meant what I said because I always speak with conviction and I don't say anything to my students that I don't mean. If I had tried to backtrack and change the intention of what I said it would have damaged my credibility and my professional integrity. I made a mistake, I accepted responsibility for it, and I apologized. That was the right thing to do and I'm sure the student respected me and trusted me more for having been honest. The academic alliance is strengthened by such circumstances.

One of my favorite lines from the movie *Top Gun* is, "A good pilot is compelled to evaluate what has happened so he can apply what he's learned." It then stands to reason that a good teacher is compelled to evaluate what has happened so he/she can apply what has been learned. And I have. Now before I hand out an exam, I never make any reference as to how easy or difficult I think it is. The actual difficulty of an exam is subjective anyway as all students have a different idea of what "difficult" means. From that point on when I hand out an exam, I simply say, "Here is the exam. Take your time, read the questions carefully, and do the best that you can."

CHAPTER TWENTY-THREE

Clinical Supplements

EVERY PSYCHOLOGY CLASS HAS a textbook. Every teacher has similar information to cover in order to satisfy the educational requirements within the state where the course is being taught. What makes one class better than another? What ultimately makes the difference between a class that students look forward to and one they dread? I am always striving to improve my teaching skills to give my students the best possible experience, so this is a question that I consistently ponder. And I found what I think is the answer.

In his extraordinary book, *Existential Psychotherapy*, Irvin Yalom tells a story about a cooking class he once took where, try as they might, he and the other students could not get their dishes to taste as good as the teacher's. Yalom went on to say, "Then I caught her throwing in extra ingredients that weren't in the recipe when she thought nobody else was looking. These gave her dishes that special flavor everyone loved."[1] Yalom made the point that throwing in extras like these are what make therapy better too. When I read this, it made sense to me that by throwing in extra topics that are not in the recipe (the treatment plan), I could customize my class to make it a more meaningful experience for my students.

When I began looking at my treatment plan from this perspective, I found there were an abundance of "extras" that I could

1. Yalom, *Existential Psychotherapy*, 3–4.

throw in "when nobody was looking" that were clinically relevant, fit into the class mission statement, and would greatly enhance the quality of my classes. I reevaluated my course treatment plan from the perspective that it was a recipe that needed a boost. Then I systematically began implementing the "clinical supplements" that my students enjoy so much. I must confess that this also enhances my experience teaching the class. Additionally, I began asking my students on the first day of class to include in the anonymous feedback any topics they would like to learn about that were not listed in the current treatment plan. This gives the students a voice and provides me with the opportunity to customize the class to meet their interests. Students will naturally be interested in a topic if they chose it.

With proper planning, I can introduce many different topics. I always leave some dates on my treatment plan where I list the topic for that day as "to be announced." This is where I throw in the "extras" when nobody is looking. Some examples are a training on relationship violence, how to identify and report child abuse, suicide prevention, and how to control one's metabolism better via strength training. This is an ongoing process. With the use of anonymous feedback, the students give me a good sense of which topics worked, which ones didn't, as well as suggestions for future topics. Trial and error are part of the process, and students enjoy helping to create the class. Collaboration equals success.

CHAPTER TWENTY-FOUR

Redefine What It Means to Be Successful
It's Not About the Grade

WE LIVE IN AN era where too much emphasis is placed on winning. It's gotten to the point where athletic teams made up of younger people sometimes receive trophies or medals when they have not achieved victory because tangible prizes have become more important than taking pride in having done one's best regardless of the outcome. There are even professional athletes who trade constantly from one team to another because the pursuit of a championship takes precedence over loyalty and longevity. Phrases like, "winning isn't everything, it's the only thing," and, "nobody remembers who came in second," fuel this way of thinking. In my opinion this is a shallow and superficial way of viewing things. For a person to mature, the reality that one will not always win must be taught and accepted. It's the only realistic way to live.

From my perspective, true victory is reflected in the effort that someone makes as opposed to the results of that effort. When I initially introduce this concept to my students, I use well-known events like the Super Bowl and the World Series as examples. I say, "two teams who are passionate, motivated, disciplined, and well-trained compete at the highest level. Even if neither team makes a single mistake or error, one of the teams is going to lose." Then I pose the following question to the class. "Who thinks the players on the team that was not victorious are losers?" Without fail, nobody raises their hand. When it is presented in that way, the students begin to see the validity in what I am driving at. Once I have the students in that frame of mind, I make the transition from athletes trying for a victory to students who are trying for an A. Then I explain how I want them to apply this logic to themselves.

I tell my students on the first day of class to consider that success is measured via making one's absolute best attempt to succeed, as opposed to the outcome of that effort. I take the winner vs. loser factor out of the equation. This becomes a powerful and useful concept in the everyday lives of the students who choose to accept this way of thinking. It does not just impact how they view what it means to be successful in my class. More importantly, it changes their perception of what it means to be successful in their lives.

When I initially present this concept in terms of how I measure success in my class, I say the following. "I don't expect everyone in this class to get an A. I do however expect each of you to do your absolute best all the time. At the end of the semester, if you can honestly say that you did your absolute best all the time, then no matter what your final grade is, you have succeeded." This brings such relief to some students. Experienced teachers know there are students in every class who, regardless of making their best effort, are simply not capable of achieving an A. Part of making the academic experience meaningful is motivating students to want to learn the material for the ultimate purpose of improving their lives and not just to earn a grade. I've had students over the years who manage to get an A in my course, but whom I'm confident have not truly learned the "life lessons" that I attempt to impart as well as other students who despite their best effort earned a B or a C.

A winning attitude is always better than a winning record. A winning record is momentary, but a winning attitude is permanent. A person with a winning attitude is more concerned with the journey than the destination. A person with a winning attitude will stay motivated. A person with a winning attitude will have a more satisfying life full of personal victories despite the possibility of never earning a trophy, a championship ring, or an A.

CHAPTER TWENTY-FIVE

Relationships Are an Investment in Your Future

ONE OF THE TECHNIQUES that I use to motivate students to effectively and objectively evaluate their lives is to share what I call motivational phrases with them. These are not meditations. These are phrases that have profound and undeniable meaning. They are thought-provoking, and thinking is the first step in making choices that are in one's best interest. One of the phrases that I use makes up the title of this chapter, "Relationships are an investment in your future."

Before I share this phrase with the students and process the meaning of it, I must get them into the proper mindset. Here is the way I always begin this conversation. I ask, "Which of you know how the stock market and retirement plans work?" Everyone raises their hand. Then I say, "Imagine I am a stock broker, and I want to sell you this stock. But before I sell it to you, I want you to know that this stock is no good. All the warning signs are present that this stock is going to tank. If you invest your money in it, you are going to go broke even though it looks very attractive. Now that you are aware of this, how many of you would like to buy my stock?" Naturally nobody raises their hands, and thus they all concede that they would not be so foolish as to invest their money in something that was most likely going to tank. Once I have confirmed this point, I go into the actual lesson that I want to teach them.

Now I instruct them to take out their notebooks and write down this phrase in first person, "My relationships are an investment in my future." Then I make the comparison between how investing one's money in the stock market to secure a happy retirement is no different than investing oneself in relationships to secure their happiness and personal fulfillment. When this comparison is made, the students are typically on board and begin to understand where I am going with this concept.

I then pose the following questions for the students to consider. I request that they don't publicly express the answers as these are private matters. "How many of you know someone, perhaps yourself, who is currently investing in a relationship that is practically guaranteed to tank?" "How many of you are investing your time and your heart in a romantic relationship with someone who mistreats you, is untrustworthy, is abusive or inattentive?" "How many of you are involved with peer groups who do things, or entice you to do things, that could get you into trouble and compromise your future?" And finally, "How many of you are in a one-sided friendship with someone who uses you when they need something, but are never there for you?" I then ask the students to give those questions some thought. I ask them to honestly evaluate the quality of their relationships and determine if they are investing wisely in their emotional futures. It's ironic, and sad I suppose, that people are more careful with how they invest their money than how they invest their hearts, physical safety, and emotional well-being.

This is one of my favorite exercises. When I have this conversation with the students, it is always productive. I can see their facial expressions change as they begin to ponder what I just presented. The painful reality of the choices they are making begins to set in. After I present this concept to my students, there are always some who disclose to me in future papers, or via anonymous feedback, that as a direct result of this exercise they have begun to re-evaluate who they invest their time in. They tell me they have begun to make healthier choices in terms of their relationships via taking a closer look at who they spend time with. A student will occasionally report having ended a destructive relationship or having avoided entering yet another one as a result of this exercise. As a teacher I find this very gratifying. Empowering students to make healthier choices is a big part of what teaching is about.

CHAPTER TWENTY-SIX

Want to Know How You Are Doing?
Request Anonymous Feedback

As a teacher I want to know as much as possible about what the students are thinking about the class, the material, and me. Is the class meeting their expectations? Is there something they would like me to do differently? Is there a topic they would like me to cover? Every semester the students complete a course evaluation for the college, but as a teacher I don't get to see that feedback until several weeks after the semester has ended. This helps me to make revisions for the next class but does nothing in terms of my goal to make things meaningful for the *current* class. To remedy this problem, I decided many years ago to start soliciting anonymous feedback from my students. I begin doing this on the very first day of class, and then continue to do it periodically throughout the semester. This technique is incredibly effective. It keeps communication open, it helps me to customize each class to best meet the needs of the students, and it strengthens the academic alliance.

At the end of the very first class, after I have reviewed the treatment plan and given my opening motivational lecture which outlines what my expectations are, what they can expect from me, etc., I begin the process of soliciting anonymous feedback. There are specific things that I want to know. I ask them for their first impression. Upon meeting me for the first time and hearing my opening lecture, what is their opinion? Are they excited about the class?

Are they nervous about the high expectations I have of them? Is the class what they were expecting? I also ask each student to tell me what he/she ultimately hopes to gain by taking the course. Since the feedback is anonymous, they are free to express anything they like without the fear of retribution that normally comes with expressing oneself. Participating in this activity is completely voluntary.

If you choose to try this technique, you may find that students are not comfortable with giving this kind of constructive and/or critical feedback to an authority figure, even anonymously. There are several possible reasons for this. First, it is likely that no other teacher has ever asked for this kind of feedback, so providing it may feel strange. Second, if a student grew up with authoritarian parents who made demands, refused to compromise, and did not allow the student to have a voice, the student may feel like she doesn't have the right to offer criticism even though the teacher asked for it. She may feel it is disrespectful to offer this kind of criticism. Remember, a teacher is symbolic of a parent. And finally, previous teachers have not overtly stated that they value the input of the students and want to collaborate with them to make the class as meaningful as possible. I have found that while the initial feedback may not be overly expressive, once the students get used to doing this, subsequent feedback is very expressive. Typically, once the students get comfortable and trust me, they will offer feedback openly in the class setting. That is a beautiful thing.

For this technique to have the desired effect, the feedback must be openly acknowledged. When I solicit for feedback at the end of class, I always begin the next class by thanking the students for their feedback and helping me to improve our academic alliance. To make sure they know I have read their comments and take them seriously, I will quote specific things that were disclosed out loud, and then explain how I am going to implement what was suggested. And equally important, if there are suggestions that for some reason I cannot implement, I explain why. Before I ask for the feedback the first time, I explain that there are some things about the class that can be changed, and some things that can't. This way, none of the students will be made to feel that their suggestions were not taken into consideration. Students come to really like the diplomatic tone this gives the class. The following is an example of how soliciting for anonymous feedback helped me to improve a class in real time.

As a teacher, I think it is important to teach from memory. To me this serves three purposes. One, it demonstrates that I have a solid knowledge of the material and that I am totally prepared for class. Two, it allows me to make eye contact with my students and talk with them as opposed to reading to them from power point slides. And three, my exams contain short answer and fill-in-the-blank questions. I think it would be hypocritical of me to expect my students to commit the material to memory if I haven't done so myself. Three weeks into a semester, I solicited for anonymous feedback and here is one response that spoke for most of the class. "Professor Bunn, I like the way that you teach from memory. It is impressive that you don't need notes. None of my other teachers do that. But I can't write as fast as you talk. By the time I write down one point, I miss the next, and I am scared I am missing important material. It would be helpful if you could use some visual aid like power point for us to follow. I understand if you don't want to, I just thought I would ask."

This proved to be very valuable feedback. I gave this matter a lot of thought and decided to honor the request. I will admit at that time, and even now, I don't like using power point or an overhead projector, but I began doing so anyway. I did this to demonstrate to the students that I do listen to them and care about their needs, and to facilitate the academic alliance. This was a great opportunity to utilize my philosophy that collaboration equals success. This one simple change created a better learning environment for these students. And I was pleasantly surprised to find that I did not have to drastically change my lecture style to make this work. I now put notes on the overhead projector so that students can write down the important terms and concepts and not fear missing something. Meanwhile, I found I can still teach from memory, make eye contact, and talk with students as opposed to reading to them. I put notes on the overhead for their benefit, but I don't use it. This turned out to be an "everybody wins" situation. I am still able to set an example of why memorizing information is important, and the visual learners have a better opportunity to succeed.

This is just one of the numerous examples I could present in terms of how soliciting for anonymous feedback during the semester is useful. The students and I collaborated to solve a problem. The students felt empowered because their voices were heard. And most importantly, I proved that I meant what I said to them on the first day of class in terms of us being equal partners helping each other to succeed. What a great feeling that is.

CHAPTER TWENTY-SEVEN

Trust: It's a Great Form of Flattery

ONE MORNING I DECIDED to play a joke on my students. The topic we were going to discuss that day was stress and the potentially negative impact it can have on one's mental and physical health. It was my thinking that the best way to get the students in the proper mindset to talk about this would be to create a stressful situation for them and then process what it felt like. Here is what I did that morning at the beginning of class to set the mood.

I said, "Good morning everyone. Please clear your desks of everything except something to write with. I have been telling you throughout the semester that it's important to study the material in between classes. Today we are going to have a surprise quiz to see how well you have been doing that." I then picked up a pile of papers and pretended that I was about to hand out an exam. Just as I was about to do that I smiled and said, "Ok, I was just kidding." We all laughed together for a moment, and then I said, "Ok. So, who was totally stressed out and nervous about having a surprise test just then?" To my astonishment no hands were raised. I then asked, "Was anyone at least just a little worried?" Once again it was a unanimous no. I then laughed and said, "Well, I guess it's a good thing that I'm not an actor. And apparently I am a bad liar too. I can't believe I didn't fool any of you."

It was at that moment a student raised her hand and said, "Professor Bunn. You are not a bad actor or a bad liar. The reason we didn't believe you were going to give us a surprise exam is because you told us on the first day of class that you would never do that. And since you have always kept your word, we trust you. If you gave us a surprise exam that would mean that you had lied to us, and we know you would never do that."

I then looked at the class and asked, "Is that the case? Is that really why none of you got even a little nervous?" It was a unanimous, "yes." What could I say? I thanked the student who spoke up and shared with me what turned out to be a great compliment. I always hope to earn the trust of my students, and this is an example of how that effort paid off. This validates that students do watch and listen to see if we teachers will be consistent, fair, and keep our word. Trust is the basis of any relationship, and a key component of establishing the academic alliance.

CHAPTER TWENTY-EIGHT

Convince Them the Class is Worth Their While

IN MY TEACHING EXPERIENCE, the opening lecture/motivational speech on the first day of class is crucial. It is essential to capture the attention of the students and spark their interest in the course from the moment the class begins. You won't get a second shot at this. Students size up a teacher on the first day of class and whoever the teacher fails to impress will either drop the class, or never totally invest in it. This does not leave much time for a teacher to get students on board for this journey, but with proper planning it can be done. I pull it off every semester, and so can you. No matter the subject, it's our job to make it meaningful to the students and get them to see the value of learning the material.

So how does a teacher go about motivating students into not just tolerating a course, but thriving on it? This is where your enthusiasm and confidence are key. This is where the teacher needs to be an effective motivational speaker. The teacher must introduce the course in a passionate manner. A credible argument must be made to the students as to why taking this course will benefit them and change their lives for the better. Students must leave the class on day one no longer just taking the course because it's required or just for a grade. They must be excited about the course because they now see it as crucial to their future success in life. The students must concede that that class is not what they expected. The teacher must convince them that by taking this course the quality of their lives will dramatically improve.

One of the classes that I teach is Introduction to Psychology. This class presents a special challenge because typically students must take this as a required core course. It is basically mandated. Therefore, it is that much more important to demonstrate the value of the course because many of the students would not take it if they didn't have to. The following are some examples of exactly what I say during my initial lecture for my Introduction to Psychology classes. I have found these remarks to be highly effective.

"If you are willing to do the work and approach this class with an open mind, I guarantee that what you learn will improve the quality of your life. I promise that if you commit yourself to working hard, at the end of the semester when we part company, you will be a better version of yourself than you are right now."

I also say, "You will learn to use the principles of psychology to effectively create the circumstances in your life that you want. You will improve your chances of being successful academically, vocationally, and socially. And the best part is you won't have to wait until some point in the future to reap the benefits of what you are going to learn here. You will be able to apply what you learn in this class to your present life. I will teach you something new in every class that you can begin to apply to your life immediately if you choose to do so. In this class you will not just learn about psychology, you will experience it and learn how to apply it. I am offering this to you as an opportunity. I am excited to present this opportunity to you, and it is my hope that you will accept it. Those of you who do will be glad you did."

I speak with conviction. The way in which I present this information captivates my students. I make the above assertions to my students because I know I can deliver. I make these promises and guarantees to my students in such a way that they not only believe me, but they also believe in me. When the course is presented in this way it excites and intrigues even those students who are initially skeptical. I tell my students directly and without any self-doubt why this class will be important to them and how it will immediately begin improving their lives. My choice of words, tone of voice, and method of delivery inspire hope and generate curiosity. Students are not used to hearing teachers make promises and guarantee results that will change their lives. I am happy to make such assertions, and I do so with confidence.

I will note here that throughout this lecture, and throughout the semester, I make sure to remind students that these results can only happen if they are responsible enough to do their part. Accountability is key. The results I speak of don't happen via osmosis. I am responsible for my behavior and for providing the students with opportunities to make positive changes. The students must do their part as well. I always remind my students that while it is very important to me that they succeed, it cannot be more important to me than it is to them. They must do the work. Ultimately, they are responsible for whatever results they achieve. Learning via school is like healing via therapy. The patient must work in between therapy sessions and put into practice in one's life what has been learned in order to see results. Likewise, students must study in between class sessions and put into practice what has been learned in class in order to see results. Teachers and therapists are like tour guides. We lead the way and point people in the right direction, but the student and/or client is ultimately responsible for making the necessary changes.

CHAPTER TWENTY-NINE

I Almost Got That Job

I INSIST THAT MY students pay attention to detail, follow directions, and read instructions carefully. Sometimes students get annoyed with me because of how strict I am about this. Through the years I've had numerous students lose points as the result of not reading exam questions carefully or not following the instructions for a writing assignment. The very first supervisor I ever had when I began working as a clinician drilled the notion of paying attention to detail into me, because I too used to overlook small things that I didn't think mattered.

Students must learn to appropriately follow through on what is being asked of them by the teacher. This is an important life lesson because eventually demands will be made of them in the workforce, and instead of losing points, there will be a risk of losing a job, losing a promotion, or perhaps receiving a poor evaluation. Supervisors always have respect for people who pay attention to detail and complete tasks appropriately. School is a place where this kind of behavior should be taught and reinforced so that it becomes second nature to the student. Allowing students to slide on this part of the process enables them and does them a tremendous disservice.

I always provide examples from my own life or clinical work to explain and validate why the lessons I am teaching are relevant to real life. The following is an example that I provide to students every semester. It's a story that I call, "I almost got that job." It validates the importance of taking the time to read directions and pay attention to details.

When I was in college, I saw an ad in the newspaper for a part-time job working at a local golf course. I liked to play golf so I thought working at a golf course would be a fun way to earn some money, not to mention getting to play golf there for free. Strangely the ad did not provide a phone number, which annoyed me. So, I looked up the number and called the club. The man who answered the phone was very nice. We talked for about fifteen minutes. At the end of the conversation he said, "Well David, you seem like someone who would have really been a good fit here. It's too bad I can't hire you." I responded, "What do you mean? You just said I would fit in well there. I don't understand." He then said, "The reason is because you called about the job. The add specifically said no phone inquiries. Apply in person." That explained why there was no phone number. "Oh, I didn't notice that. But since we talked can't I at least have an interview?" He said, "David, taking care of a golf course requires the ability to pay attention to details. You missed a very important detail that was boldly stated in the ad. How can I trust that you will be more careful here? It was a pleasure speaking to you, and good luck."

In that moment I was angry at the man I spoke to on the phone. How could he be so rigid? This is not fair. However, once I calmed down and thought about it, I realized the person I was really angry with was myself. He was right. I missed an important detail. When I tell this story to my students, besides finding it funny, they gain a better understanding of why paying attention to detail is important, and how failing to do so has the potential to be costly.

CHAPTER THIRTY

The Gratitude Letter

I THINK IT IS important that the writing assignments that students do have some personal meaning to them as well as a connection to the course material. To come up with assignments like these requires creativity on the part of the teacher, and a desire to learn more about the students. In his book *Staring at the Sun*, Irvin Yalom mentions an exercise that he learned during a workshop he attended many years ago from a gentleman named Martin Seligman. It was called the "Gratitude Visit." Yalom makes the point that, "too often people express posthumous gratitude."[1] This type of gratitude is typically offered to people in the form of eulogies when they are not able to hear it." The point is that we should express gratitude to those in our lives who deserve it *while they are alive to hear it.*

When I read about this, I knew I had come across a life-changing exercise. It motivated me to begin writing gratitude letters to the people I care about and to whom I owed a debt of thanks. I want the people who mean something to me to know it while they are alive and can feel good about the way they have impacted my life. I wrote such a letter to my father a few years before he died. I have also written such letters to my mother as well as a doctor with

1. Yalom, *Staring at the Sun*, 135.

whom I had a special relationship. I have many more such letters to write. And this is a win-win situation. The people who receive the letters always feel great, and I must admit it feels wonderful to give people the letters. I owe Irvin Yalom a debt of gratitude for passing along Martin Seligman's exercise. In my opinion Irvin Yalom is the greatest psychiatrist and writer of our time. I highly recommend to the readers of this book that you read each of his.

I had already been teaching at the college level for ten years when I read about this exercise. In addition to incorporating this into my own life, I immediately began using this as an assignment in my classes. Early in each semester, I require my students to choose one person whom they know personally and who had a positive impact on his/her life. I then ask the students to write a gratitude letter to that person. The letter cannot be a superficial, just-going-through-the-motions exercise. To receive credit for the assignment the student must reference specific examples and reasons as to why this person has made such a difference to them. Students often say, "I didn't realize how many people in my life have helped me until I was forced to pick just one."

The way I lead into this assignment is, "So many times in life we assume that the people to whom we are most grateful, know it. Unfortunately, most of the time people who have been so generous to us don't realize it because this is just their way. They think everyone behaves like this so there is nothing special about them. How tragic it is that such wonderful people may go to their graves never knowing how much we really appreciate them." Then I explain the assignment. Additionally, I read aloud to the class an example of a gratitude letter that I wrote to give the students an idea of what I want them to do.

Students respond very positively to this assignment. The feedback that I get from them is always meaningful and emotionally charged. Students often report that once they choose a person and start writing, suddenly they remember even more things this person has said or done that were helpful. The floodgates open and memories start coming back. I've had students report tearing up or crying while writing these letters. The task takes on a life of its own. It goes from being an assignment being done for a grade, to a heart-felt task that allows students to truly experience the power of altruism in the form of gratitude. It motivates students to open their eyes to a new perspective on their lives and the people who have played a crucial role in them.

I don't require students to share the contents of their letters with each other because they often write about very private things that nobody else should know. We do process what it was like to write the letters as a class, and that is always a great conversation. Students report that the assignment was meaningful, and they enjoyed doing it. I've even had students say, "At first I thought this assignment was kind of a waste of time. But when I sat down and started doing it, I was pleasantly surprised about how much I liked it." I also don't require the students to send the letters. However, most do, and then report back to me via anonymous feedback how happy it made them to give the letter, and more importantly, how thrilled and surprised the recipient of the letter was to get it.

After the class is finished processing how it felt to write the letter, we move on to the next part of the assignment. This entails a question that I pose to the group. I do not require anyone to answer this question aloud. I just want them to think about it. This last task is an important part of the lesson and should always be done. Here is what I say as we are wrapping this up. "Now that you have experienced this assignment, I want you all to consider the following question. If I were to seek out the people in your lives, those that make up your families and peer groups, and gave them this assignment, do you think any of them would choose to write about you?" "And if not, why not?" "What changes do you need to make in terms of how you treat others, such that years from now, people in your life will want to write a gratitude letter to you?" This always makes the students think about how they behave, how they treat other people, and how they are living their lives. It's a great question, and feedback I receive from the students usually consists of statements like this one. "Professor Bunn, after you posed the question about whether anyone in my life would write me a gratitude letter, sadly I concluded they wouldn't. While I initially felt upset about this, it motivated me to change my ways and be more thoughtful of other people. Thank you for having us do this assignment. I would not have seen how selfish I have been had we not done this."

In addition to raising self-awareness, this assignment helps to facilitate the academic alliance. Within these letters, students often share very personal information about themselves that assists me with creating what I call therapeutic lectures. I discuss therapeutic lectures later in the book. Over the years, students have used these letters to talk about illnesses they have, divorces they've survived, addictions they are struggling with, abuse they have endured, mental illnesses they are battling, etc. Their willingness to share such information with me is demonstrative of trust. If you are a teacher who does not want to know intimate details about your student's lives, then don't do this assignment.

I always express my gratitude to my students for completing this assignment, and for trusting me with personal information about their lives. I commend the students for how strong they are, and for how well they have endured the various challenges that have already come up in their young lives. I express that I have learned things about life from what they have shared and their wisdom. Students like knowing they taught me something. It increases their self-worth and validates that I respect them. This is an assignment that I usually give on the second day of class. The emotionally charged impact it has sets the tone for the rest of the semester. When a student is emotionally invested in the academic alliance, it's a beautiful thing.

CHAPTER THIRTY-ONE

The Self-Talk Evaluation Paper

THINKING IS A HABIT. And just like any other habit it can be healthy or destructive. Throughout the semester I frequently discuss with my students how powerful their thoughts are, and how their thoughts have a definitive impact on how they feel. Most people, unless they have been in therapy with someone who subscribes to cognitive behavioral techniques, have not taken the time to track and analyze their thought patterns. As I mentioned earlier, there is no substitute for experience. To provide my students with an opportunity to really understand their own thought patterns, I assign what I call the self-talk evaluation paper.

This is a very simple assignment. I ask my students to pick just one day of the week and write down as many of their thoughts that day as they can in bullet form. I ask them to pick twenty-five or thirty of the most powerful thoughts from that day and examine them for patterns. They are to look for patterns of negativity, positivity, anxiety, any cognitive distortions that might be present, as well as any defense mechanisms. Next, they are to list each statement separately and write a corresponding paragraph which explains how that thought impacted their feelings and behavior that day. And finally, they are to write a summary of what they learned from this experience. In my experience, students are so confident in their self-awareness that expectations of learning something from this are low. This is one time where low expectations are welcome because students are always amazed by what they learn about themselves, and not having expected to learn anything magnifies the impact of the experience.

Here are some of the typical comments that students make in their summaries. "I didn't realize how negative my thoughts really are." "I noticed I beat myself up a lot." "I spend more time worrying than I thought I did." Ultimately, after making these honest observations, students will go on to say how they are now going to make the effort to think more positively, worry less, lighten up on themselves a little. For people to be successful, their habits of thinking need to focus more on victory and success. This exercise illuminates for students the impact of their thoughts in a powerful and meaningful way.

CHAPTER THIRTY-TWO

The Wake-Up Call

THIS IS AN EXISTENTIAL writing assignment that I came across via Irvin Yalom. He refers to an awakening experience as, "one in which a person undergoes a transformation. Experiences like these can take the form of a confrontation with death that enriches life, a significant birthday, the death of a loved one, or any other experience that makes one aware of his/her mortality and more primed to make significant changes."[1] When I came across this idea, I knew immediately this was something that I needed to incorporate in my classes.

I want my students to appreciate the time they have. I want them to guard against taking life for granted, and to begin living now at a young age with a greater sense of urgency. Yalom referenced the famous movie, *A Christmas Carol*, and the transformation that Scrooge ultimately goes through after his experience in the cemetery, with the Ghost of Christmas Yet to Come. This is a perfect lead-in.

To prepare my students for this assignment, I begin by showing the part of *A Christmas Carol* where Scrooge is visited by the three spirits. I don't tell them why I am doing this. I stop the movie after Scrooge demonstrates significant life changes after the Ghost

1. Yalom, *Staring at the Sun*, 31–32.

of Christmas Yet to Come, essentially the Grim Reaper, warns him of his impending death if he does not change his ways.

At that point I explain to the students that what they just saw was a powerful example of an "awakening experience." Showing that part of the movie is a great way to get students in the proper mindset for understanding the assignment I am about to give. Additionally, it's an entertaining film which remarkably some students have never seen.

I then instruct them that I want each of them to carefully examine their lives and pick out something that would qualify as an "awakening experience." I point out that while it could be a brush with death, it doesn't have to be. Positive things qualify as life changing experience as well. For example, I have a friend who upon the birth of his first child, sold his motorcycle, quit smoking, and began working out. His experience was not generated by a brush with death, but to the contrary, a brush with life. When his child was born his priorities changed and he began living differently. He wanted to stay healthy to watch his daughter grow up, graduate high school, get married, etc.

I've had several "awakening experiences" in my own life, and I share them with my students. The death of my father, my brother's deployment during the Gulf War, and a near miss on my Harley are just a few. All of these served to put me in a position to realize how fragile life is, how quickly time passes by, and how important it is to live as fully as possible in the present moment.

Once I have done that, I explain to my students that in addition to being motivated to live with a greater sense of urgency upon having an "awakening experience" is to remember not to go back to sleep. When I make that assertion, I get strange looks, so I use an example to clarify what I mean.

Many years ago, I knew someone who had a massive heart attack. He'd had no history of heart trouble, but he was a very heavy smoker who didn't exercise. He survived and recovered from the heart attack. But the experience scared him. The sudden difficulty breathing, the crushing pain in his chest, and the fear of death shook him up. He decided to make some drastic yet positive life changes. He quit smoking, he started exercising, and ate a better diet. Sounds great right?

I ran into him five months after this happened and we began talking. A few minutes into the conversation he lit up a cigarette. He went "back to sleep." It is not uncommon for people to go back to their old ways once the emotional impact and the memory of what happened fades away. The "awakening experience" loses its power if we don't strive to make positive and permanent life changes as a result of them. I recommend that people write down the emotional content of the life changing experience so when time causes it to lose its force, one can be reminded about the feeling via reading about it, and avoid going back to sleep.

CHAPTER THIRTY-THREE

The Empathy Paper

EMPATHY IS A MISUNDERSTOOD concept outside of the mental health field. Sometimes even people who work in the field forget what empathy is and how to demonstrate it. I frequently hear mental health professionals casually say, "I know exactly how you feel." That is a key difference between people who live psychology, and those who strictly do it for a living. I have not said the phrase, "I know exactly how you feel" since I was an undergrad in college and learned not to do that.

Before we part company at the end of the semester, all my students are aware of what empathy is and how to demonstrate it properly. One of the misconceptions about empathy is that to demonstrate it, one must have had the same experience as someone else. This is not true. The goal of empathy is to identify with the feeling the person is experiencing, not the experience itself. Naturally there will be times when one has the same, or at least a similar, experience as someone else. Even then it's still inappropriate to say, "I know exactly how you feel." An empathic response involving a similar experience would be, "After my car accident I had a difficult time driving for a while. How did your accident impact you?" Or, "I felt a sense of relief after my divorce. How are you feeling about the end of your marriage?" In both these statements, the speaker presents as having a similar experience, offers how he/she felt about it, and then inquires as to how the person being spoken to is feeling. The other person is not robbed of his/her uniqueness. Perfect.

Since identifying with the feelings of others is the goal, everyone can demonstrate accurate and appropriate empathy. The variety of feelings that people experience is made up of anger, joy, fear, betrayal, grief, love, hate, sadness, and powerlessness. So as a therapist, if I am talking to someone who is angry, I don't have to identify with the person's experience, I just need to remember what it feels like to be angry, and then I can make the connection. It's not that complicated and it's very effective. I sometimes say something like, "I haven't experienced what you have, but I've had experiences in my life that have made me angry. What is it like for you?" In this case I did not pretend to have the same experience, but I did assert that I can identify with the feeling. Being able to do this is a great communication skill and I think everyone should learn it. My students do.

For this assignment I ask the students to choose an experience that generated a strong emotional response. I ask them to write the story about it, identify the feeling, and then answer the following questions. What was it like to feel this way? How did this impact your decision making? Did this impact your worldview and values? What did you learn from this? Did anyone try to help you? Do you have any regrets about your behavior during this time?

Students enjoy this assignment, and this is one where I learn a lot about their life experiences and they way they think. The idea here is to teach them the power of a feeling, not any specific feeling. They get to choose. Then I tell them to remember this feeling when they are talking to someone else who may have had a different experience, but the same feeling, and use that to connect and empathize with the person. By teaching students to do this with one feeling, they can make the leap to understanding how to do it with the entire variety of feelings that people have. It's a great lesson and the feedback I get from students about it is very positive.

CHAPTER THIRTY-FOUR

Papers Are a Vehicle for Catharsis

In clinical terms, catharsis refers to the feeling of relief that one gets from talking about things or, "getting something off one's chest." That kind of relief is therapeutic and is always part of what a therapist is trying to achieve with a client during a round of therapy.

Since my philosophy is that the classroom is a therapeutic milieu and that learning is a form of therapy, it stands to reason that providing students with opportunities for "catharsis"-like experiences is something I strive to do. I don't overtly share with my students that this is what I am hoping for. When it happens it's the natural result of a genuine and trusting relationship in which personal information is shared in a safe environment. Establishing a relationship and creating an environment in which students feel comfortable sharing such information is a challenge. That is why I spend so much time cultivating the "academic alliance" referenced earlier in the book. Once that is established, amazing things happen.

In a traditional therapeutic relationship, there is privacy and one-on-one conversations. In a classroom setting these components are not possible. And from an academic standpoint, while I consider office hours to be therapeutic due to the active problem solving and "academic therapy" that takes place, it is *not* psychotherapy. Even therapists like myself who also teach are not allowed to provide psychotherapy, so I don't. However, it is possible to create opportunities for catharsis in the academic setting, and I do so via the self-reflective writing assignments that I have students do. This is a safe way to do this because students have total control over the process. Students who are comfortable sharing personal details of their lives do so. Students who are not comfortable doing so complete the assignment on a more superficial level, which is perfectly fine. Lack of disclosure does not impact their grade.

My thinking on this issue once again is consistently validated by my students via feedback that I receive. Some examples of feedback that I get regarding my choice of writing assignments which indicate catharsis, despite students not calling it that, are the following.

"This was my favorite paper. It was tough but it forced me to look at a situation I had been hiding from. I felt relieved after writing about it" (catharsis). "You are the only person I have told about this. I have been carrying this around for a long time, and I'm glad I got it out of my system" (catharsis). And one more. "I had long since forgotten about this experience. When you gave this assignment, it jarred my memory. Writing about this made me feel good" (catharsis).

When students write the papers I spoke of earlier, they enjoy the process. Everyone's favorite topic, whether they admit it or not, is themselves. I overtly tell my students on the first day of class, "The writing assignments that I give are going to force you to take an honest look at yourself and your life. I am giving you permission to be narcissistic for the next fifteen weeks. The class mission statement is to get to know yourself better, and the writing assignments will help you to do that."

A word of caution about the writing assignments listed in this book. If you are a teacher who is uncomfortable learning intimate and emotionally charged details about the lives of your students, then don't give these assignments. I have found that even though some students remain guarded and superficial in their completion of these assignments, most don't. Most students enthusiastically share things about themselves. They are happy that someone has taken an interest in their lives, and they enjoy the personal growth that comes from honest self-reflection.

CHAPTER THIRTY-FIVE

When the "Academic Illness" is Terminal

TYPICALLY, WHEN THE WORD terminal is used, people think of terminal illness. But terminal is a word that refers to the imminent and inevitable ending of something. All endings are symbolic of death. As a therapist I have worked with people who are coping with a terminal illness as well as other terminal conditions like the ending of a marriage via divorce, the termination of parental rights as a result of abuse, or the termination of a job via retirement, to name a few. Irvin Yalom has done extensive clinical work with patients who are dying from a terminal illness. Yalom makes the assertion that, "one can offer no greater service to someone facing death than to offer your sheer presence."[1]

So, what is the academic illness and when is it terminal? This is a concept that I use to refer to that point in time at the end of the semester when a student is going to fail the course or receive a grade that is not satisfactory to him/her. I consider this a terminal condition because there is a definitive negative outcome. It is too late for the student to drop the course, and there is no more effective treatment available in the form of papers and exams to cure it. It's over and now there's just a countdown to when final grades are

1. Yalom, *Staring at the Sun*, 125.

submitted. All teachers have students who experience this condition. Students who care suffer when they find themselves in this position and the reality of the situation sets in. As a teacher who cares about the emotional well-being of his students, when they suffer, I suffer too. When this happens, all I have left to offer in terms of support is my shear presence.

As a teacher, I have found the most difficult part of the job is knowing someone has tried their best and is not going to succeed. I have spent a good number of office hours with students who wanted to meet upon finding themselves in this situation. Initially they want to talk. This is usually a conversation where the student goes through the stages of grief.

The student may express anger and blame me for the situation. Then bargaining usually happens in the form of the question, "Can I do a paper for extra credit to improve my grade?" Ultimately, we get to the final stage of grief where acceptance (about the grade) occurs, and a moment or two of silent reflection takes place. As a therapist I am comfortable sitting with silence. Allowing someone the silent time to collect his/her thoughts is powerful. Offering my sheer presence in those moments is therapeutic. Students appreciate it when a teacher is willing to empathically go through that process with them. It's a lesson in and of itself.

CHAPTER THIRTY-SIX

Can You Defend That in Court?

TEACHING IS A JOB that requires one to behave appropriately all the time. During the twenty-six years I've spent working in the field of human services, I have been fortunate in many ways. I've had amazing supervisors whom have shared their knowledge with me and taught me lessons early in my career that have benefitted me infinitely. One of the most valuable lessons was how to communicate effectively with clients, students, etc. about sensitive clinical issues without running the risk of getting into trouble.

During a meeting with one of my supervisors over twenty years ago, I was expressing concern about how to discuss emotionally charged issues with clients without being misunderstood or getting into trouble. This is what he said. "David, I have been working in the field of human services for many years, and I've never had a legal problem. Here is why. Before I do, say, or write anything, I always ask myself the following question. Can I defend this in court? If I can't imagine myself successfully defending my actions in court under cross examination, then I make a different choice. This mindset has kept me safe throughout my entire career, and if you follow it, you will stay safe too."

This was some of the best advice I have ever received. From that day forward I have always followed that protocol and it has never failed me. I share it with all my students too. There must be a definitive clinical purpose to everything we do, say, and write, in the field of human services. If you can't imagine yourself being able to justify what you are about to do in court under cross examination, you should choose another course of action. I use this protocol when I am providing therapy to clients and when I am interacting with students. This strategy ensures that I don't act impulsively, and that I always take the time to think things through. This simple yet powerful piece of advice has kept me safe. Perhaps it will keep you safe as well. Consider this, could the teacher I referred to in chapter 1 truly justify physically pulling me out of my chair and screaming in my face in court? I doubt it.

CHAPTER THIRTY-SEVEN

Never Weigh in
On the Opinion of Parents

EARLY IN MY TEACHING career, a student asked what I thought of advice his mother had given him in terms of how to handle an academic symptom he was having. I objectively said, "I understand your mother's perspective, but there are probably other ways to look at this as well." That is all I said. At the time the comment seemed innocent enough. I was wrong. I did not stop to consider that he might share this conversation with his mother, or for what purpose. It turned out he did share it with his mother and seemingly took what I said out of context for his own benefit. The tone of her response indicated that apparently, he used my comment to show his mother that he was right and, "even Professor Bunn thinks you are wrong." The next day I received a brief but forceful e-mail from his mother which in part read, "With all due respect Professor Bunn, it's not your place to give your opinion on issues between my son and me. I'm not sure what he told you, but I would appreciate it if you would stick to teaching and leave the parenting to me." I will never know what kind of conflict I found myself in the middle of, but clearly the scope of this was much greater than the student let on during our conversation.

She was right. I made a mistake and knew it. I wrote back to her and offered a sincere apology. I did not attempt to explain my position because I thought she might interpret this as my trying to invalidate her feelings. Taking full responsibility for this was the right thing to do. Whenever I make a mistake, I process what happened so as not to make it again. I spent a lot of time trying to think of what I should have said instead. Then it occurred to me. In this case my mistake was not that I made the wrong comment. My mistake was choosing to make a comment at all. When the student asked me what I thought of his mother's perspective I should have realized there was no "safe" opinion to give, and as such not offered one.

Now I have what I call a "standard response," for situations like these. When students ask what I think about matters pertaining to personal relationships, I always say the same thing, "that is very personal and it's not my place to offer an opinion on that. It would be more productive for us to process how you feel about it." Lesson learned.

CHAPTER THIRTY-EIGHT

Student Evaluations: Read Them

THROUGH THE YEARS I have heard more than one teacher admit to not taking the time to read student evaluations. The rationalization here is typically something like, "They are all pretty much the same. I can't please everyone, so I just do what I do." It is my thinking that ignoring student evaluations is not only irresponsible, but also prevents teachers from discovering valuable data.

I read all student evaluations religiously. In fact, I can't wait to read them. Every semester I attempt to be a better teacher than I was the semester before. Student evaluations are an integral part of this process. My attitude is, I can't fix it if I don't know what's broken. And I can't find out what's broken unless I read the student evaluations.

At the end of every semester, when it is time for students to do their formal evaluations for the college, here is my scripted speech. "You have given me anonymous feedback several times during the semester that only I see. Now is your opportunity to tell the college directly what you thought of the content of the class, and what you thought of me as a teacher. I value your opinions very much and I can't improve as a teacher without your help. Please be as critical of me as possible. Be clear about anything you did not like, any expectations that were not met, and anything you think I can improve upon. While compliments are nice, criticism is better, so let me have it and don't pull your punches. Thank you." Then I leave the room as per protocol and wait in the hallway while they complete this task.

I have found the best way to utilize student evaluations for the purpose of self-improvement is to look for patterns. I call this "teacher pathology." If one or two people out of a group of thirty have an issue with something, while the other twenty-eight people did not mention it, then I conclude it is probably more their issue than mine. If five or more students out of a group of thirty point out an issue, that gives me something to think about. That motivates me to consider what I need to improve upon.

Between the formal evaluations that students do for the college, and the anonymous feedback that I request throughout the semester, I put myself in a great position to be aware of my strengths and weaknesses. No matter how experienced a teacher is, there is always room for improvement. We teachers, especially those who have been teaching for many years, must take care to remain humble, avoid complacency, and strive for continued improvement because our students deserve the best.

CHAPTER THIRTY-NINE

Avoid Diagnosing Your Students or People They Know

AFTER FACILITATING A DISCUSSION about mental illness which included the diagnostic criteria for several of them, a student approached me after class and said, "My girlfriend acts like that a lot. She shows most of the symptoms you talked about. Do you think she has depression?"

Every practicing clinician who teaches a psychology class has been asked questions like that. Students ask me that question on a regular basis. It's easy to understand why. First, most people will display the symptoms of a mental health disorder on occasion. When a student learns the diagnostic criteria for a common mental illness, i.e., major depression or obsessive compulsive disorder, it is natural for the student to suspect someone he knows, perhaps even himself, has the problem. Secondly, my students know I am a clinician. It makes sense that a student would provide me with some observations about someone he/she knows, and then ask me to confirm a diagnosis.

Every clinician knows a diagnosis cannot be made this way. It is not possible to diagnose someone with a mental health condition based exclusively on secondary evidence. And even if it could be done, it would not be appropriate for a clinician to do this as it pertains to a student or someone the student knows. When I get this question my standard answer is, "It is not possible or ethical for me to make an assessment like that under these conditions. If you have concerns, you will need to have this addressed by an independent mental health professional."

You might be thinking to yourself right now, "why don't you tell your students before you cover this material that you can't diagnose a student or someone the student knows?" The answer: I do tell them ahead of time. It doesn't matter. The question comes anyway, which is why I have prepared a standard answer.

CHAPTER FORTY

It's A Human Encounter
What Do You Have to Offer?

IT'S USEFUL FOR STUDENTS to see a teacher as more than just a person with a degree who is going to teach a class. Share yourself with your students appropriately. What more is there to your life than being a teacher? What are your interests and hobbies? What other skills do you have? What kind of music do you listen to? Do you play a sport or an instrument? What kind of movies do you enjoy? Who is your favorite team? Students will find it easier to connect with you provided you give them something to connect with. Finding things to talk about in addition to school material brings people closer together.

I share the following things about myself during the semester as opportunities to do so arise. I play the guitar. I practice martial arts. I enjoy exercise. I was a baseball player. Clint Eastwood is my favorite actor. I love watching football. I enjoy rock concerts. I ride a Harley and drive a sports car. My father was a firefighter. My brother is a Marine and a retired federal agent. My favorite writer is Irvin Yalom. I cope with my own depression. I still have a habit of procrastinating. I enjoy playing golf and bowling.

All these details about my life are appropriate to share and serve to strengthen the relationship that I have with my students. If I attend a concert during the semester, I share that. If play a great round of golf, or a horrible round of golf, I share that. At various times during the semester I start the class by asking the following questions, "Does anyone have any good news to share?" "Did anyone do anything exciting over the weekend?" Typically, students report things like having had a birthday, winning at a collegiate event, attending a wedding, etc. Students enjoy sharing these kinds of things. This sharing has nothing to do with academics, but it has everything to do with facilitating our relationship. It provides students with an opportunity to learn things about each other and me. It demonstrates that I have an interest in what is going on in their lives outside of class.

This technique of taking some time to share interesting and safe details about our lives with each other is an example of one of those "extras" that I referred to in an earlier chapter. It is a process that takes only a few moments, but it has long reaching implications. It clearly helps to facilitate and strengthen the academic alliance between the students and myself.

CHAPTER FORTY-ONE

Use Emotional Precautions
Most People Have Been Wounded

AS A FULL-TIME THERAPIST in the field of human services, I am required to take courses in first-aid, C.P.R., and how to properly use an A.E.D. Despite not being a first responder or a medical provider, therapists like myself are required to take these courses because if a client has a medical emergency we are expected to respond and provide treatment until paramedics arrive. Contained within these courses is one consistent message, and that is to always use universal precautions. Obviously, this is done because we typically don't know someone's complete medical history. Therefore, we must treat everyone as if there might be an infectious disease present to protect ourselves.

As a college teacher I don't have access to my student's records. I don't know who has a mental illness, who has been sexually assaulted, whose parents are divorced, who has an addiction, etc. I am not aware initially of who might have a learning disability, low self-esteem, or test anxiety. From my twenty-one years of teaching experience, I know that contained within every group of students are people dealing with problems like these. I know this because the students tell me about these issues via the writing assignments, office hour conversations, etc.

It is for this reason that I use what I call emotional universal precautions. I treat all my students as if they are wounded. Doing this motivates me to remember that people are fragile. Remember, they are not just students. They have lives and histories that may include significant problems. I am careful to treat the students with respect and compassion. I always create a safe environment for them in which to learn.

The main difference between the physical (barrier oriented) universal precautions that medics use, and the emotional (relationship building) precautions that I use is the following. The medically driven universal precautions create a barrier between the provider and the patient to *prevent* the provider from being exposed to the patient's problem. The emotional universal precautions that I use tear down the barrier that exists between the students and myself and *allow* me to be exposed to whatever emotional problem the student may be having. Without such exposure, the corrective academic experience cannot take place.

When I interact with students, I always use the four therapeutic factors from Carl Rogers, which are empathy, genuineness, unconditional positive regard, and active listening. When these are used properly, a safe environment is created, and students feel comfortable disclosing and talking about problems they are having. And to be clear, these conversations are therapeutic, but they are not therapy. Teachers cannot provide therapy to the students. This issue is addressed in another chapter. I think it is great when disclosures are made because it provides me with a better understanding of a student's life experience. Once I understand these things, I can proactively provide some relief via therapeutic lectures which address issues a student may be having on a universal level and provide some healing through education.

But much like the case with medical patients, I know that I will have students in my classes who have problems which I will never be made aware of. They are wounded but won't make me aware of it. It is for this reason that I use emotional universal precautions with all students. I want them all to feel safe, supported, and comfortable in my classes whether they are wounded or not.

CHAPTER FORTY-TWO

Give Students Your Résumé to Establish Credibility

PSYCHOLOGY IS A SPECIAL field. It is one that transcends the strictly academic environment. When students take a psychology course with a seasoned clinician, they expect to be exposed to the "real thing." They want to hear stories about people, things, and situations that the clinician has dealt with. To gain credibility with students I have found it be effective to tell them about my career, to give them my resume.

I don't mean that I literally print out a copy of my resume and hand it out. What I do mean is that I think it is important on the first day of class for the teacher to tell the students what his/her professional experience in the field entails. Hopefully the teacher has some. By doing this, credibility is established. When a teacher who has practical experience explains how a technique works, how to handle a crisis, what a psychiatric emergency looks like in real life, etc., students will be more prone to believe what they are being told and remember it.

On the first day of class, I tell my students how long I have worked in the field as a therapist and as an adjunct instructor. I tell them various agencies I have worked for, job titles I have held, and the various client populations I have worked with. Additionally, I tell the students all the various courses I have taught.

When I do this I always explain why. I tell the students that I am sharing this information with them because they are paying a lot of money to learn about psychology and I want them to know exactly what my experience is and what I have to offer them. Students know that teachers have academic credentials. That is a given, so I don't spend time on that. Academic credentials do not interest, educate, or motivate students. Experience does. Tell them what you have done, and whenever possible use examples from your professional experience to illuminate the material and maintain the interest of your students.

CHAPTER FORTY-THREE

A Discussion About Stress

A GOOD COMEDIAN ALWAYS has a great lead in such that the audience does not see the joke coming. This always makes the joke funnier and puts the audience in the necessary mindset just before the punch line, such that they cannot deny the validity of what was said. They have already demonstrated a specific feeling or perspective by laughing and now must take responsibility for it.

I have found that teaching the principles of psychology works in a similar fashion. It is often necessary to get students into a specific mindset, and then, when they are not expecting it, make the point. By taking them by surprise, I eliminate their ability to make up their minds about a theory, principle, or concept before I have a chance to make my point. I take away their ability to be pre-emptively skeptical.

Here is an example of how I use a lead-in when I talk about stress. Without announcing to the class what I am going to be discussing, I do a very brief activity with them which I call "point to the object." For example, I will say to the group, "please point to the clock." Then I will say, "please point to the door." And then finally, "please point to the ceiling." This is a brief exercise because by the time I ask them to point to the third object they have had enough.

Just as the students are becoming visibly frustrated and confused about this because they don't understand the purpose, I then say, "Ok. Now please point to stress." The students look around the room, they look at me, they look at each other, but nobody points to anything. Then I repeat the request and say, "You pointed to everything else, now please just point to stress for me." Once again, everyone looks confused. Then I say, "You can't point to it can you?" All agree they can't. Now comes the meaning. I then say, "You can't point to stress because it does not really exist. It does not exist that is, until you choose to create it." Upon my saying that, their eyes light up, they focus, and I have their complete attention.

If I had just come out and said, "Stress does not exist until you create it," the message would have lost its thunder. However, since everyone in the class just conceded that they could not identify stress, as per their inability to point it out, they had to admit that my point was valid. They had to admit that stress cannot be pointed out because it does not exist until they choose to create it. That simple exercise always serves as a mechanism which helps students realize how much control they have in terms of how they choose to perceive events, and the power of that perception. Having established this, I then lead a meaningful discussion on this topic by saying, "Now that we have established that stress is a product of your own creation, I want you to think about if you are choosing to be stressed out, and if so, why are you making that choice?"

I use lead-ins like this often. I used a similar lead-in earlier in the book in the chapter about relationships being an investment in one's future. I found introducing topics this way to be an amazingly effective strategy that puts students in a position to see the course material differently. It brings the material to life via practical application. It empowers students to evaluate the way they think and to consider the impact these choices have on their lives. Exercises like this excite students and motivate them to look forward to future classes with anticipation of what will happen next.

CHAPTER FORTY-FOUR

I Was A Student Once Too

STUDENTS MAKE MISTAKES. SOME mistakes are understandable, and some leave we teachers scratching our heads and saying to ourselves, "How could this have possibly happened?" I've had many such instances over the years. These situations present special challenges. For me the main challenge is to determine how I can ensure that showing some latitude is not going to do anything more than reinforce irresponsible behavior. Every teacher faces these kinds of issues, and the bottom line is every teacher must use his/her judgment to determine the best course of action on a case-by-case basis.

Here is one such example. One semester I had given a final writing assignment out four weeks before the semester was over. This was enough time to complete it. I had given out a detailed instruction sheet in class and reminded students about the deadline for the assignment in class at least twice. The end of the semester came and went, and this student did not hand in the paper. This heavily impacted his final grade, and when he saw his final grade posted on the college website, he was concerned. He sent me an e-mail and inquired about his grade. I wrote back and explained the reason for his grade was that he did not hand in the final paper, and the subsequent zero he received heavily impacted his final grade.

This student wrote back once more and said, "I didn't know about the assignment. Can I hand it in now?" How could this be, I wondered? The other fifty students knew about it. Was this a manipulative tactic? This was not the most responsible student. His attendance in the class could have been better and he often seemed distracted when he was there. Perhaps he really did manage to miss this. Before I had a chance to write back to him with an answer, he took the initiative to complete the assignment and sent it to me. He did this without knowing if I would accept it or not, and he did a great job. That I respected.

I thought it over and here is what I wrote back to him. "I have given the matter some thought and decided to accept your final paper late. Out of fairness to the people who handed it in on time it will be penalized accordingly. It is my hope that you have learned something from this, as not all teachers would be as compassionate with you under the circumstances. However, I was a student once too. I know people make mistakes, and an oversight can happen. I expect that you will not put yourself in this position again."

He wrote back and said, "Professor Bunn, thank you for letting me complete the assignment and hand it in late with a penalty. You have been more than fair with me, and I have learned my lesson. I won't let this happen again." I believed him. It is my hope that not only will he not put himself in this position again, but also that he will remember this and show kindness to someone else who perhaps needs some compassion from him upon making a mistake.

CHAPTER FORTY-FIVE

You Won't Reach Everyone

I OFTEN CONVEY TO my students that one must be very careful about how to measure success. It would be great if our best efforts always generated the desired outcome, but this is not realistic. To me success lies in the effort of doing one's best, not in the outcome. As a teacher, it is my intention to reach every student and I do my best to accomplish this. There was a time much earlier in my career as a teacher, that if I didn't reach everyone, I beat myself up. I felt like I had failed in some way. During the first several years that I taught, if a student dropped the class, I took it very personally and wondered what was wrong with me. What didn't this student like about me?

This is no longer the case. Years of experience have taught me that no matter what I do, there will be students that I will not connect with. There will be students who come to class the first day and upon hearing my opening remarks decide not to come back. There are also students who do come back and go through the motions. These students go through the motions and despite earning a good grade, there is no genuine connection. The key here is that I always do my part, and since every relationship has two responsible parties, I no longer hold myself responsible for the student's part.

From a cognitive behavioral perspective, there are several plausible explanations as to why I may not be able to reach and/or connect with a student. Here are some examples of such explanations. The student may not be interested in psychology and is there out of necessity. The student may be experiencing transference, and I remind him/her of an authority figure from their past that brings about a negative response to me. The student has personal problems and upon hearing about how self-reflective my course is, decides this is not the right place to be. And there may be a variety of other reasons too. Ultimately the message here is, you won't reach everyone, don't take it personally.

CHAPTER FORTY-SIX

The Benefit of Continuity

IN TRADITIONAL THERAPY, CONTINUITY from one session to another is desirable. It makes sense and allows for a steady transition from week to week. Most therapists, the ones that I have seen for treatment as well, typically begin a session by briefly reviewing the discussion from the previous session, and then asking a question like, "What is on your front burner right now?" Or perhaps, "What immediate concerns do you have today?" Beginning a session like that essentially puts the client in control. It allows the client to take responsibility for the session and take it where he/she wants it to go.

The classroom environment I create is run the same way. Despite that we have many topics that must get covered, I always start my classes the way my therapists have started my sessions. I always begin by saying to the class, "Before we get into today's conversation, tell me what is on your minds. How are you feeling? What questions or concerns do you have for me? What are you worried about right now that I can address with the group?" Sometimes there are questions or concerns, and sometimes there aren't. Either way is fine. But by starting the class this way, I give the students an opportunity to direct the class anywhere they want it to go. We can talk about anything they like. Once we get past that, I then do a quick review of the material we covered the class before, and then we move in to the new material. Additionally, I show a genuine interest in their emotional well-being. This matters.

Inquiring as to how students are feeling and taking a genuine interest in what is on their minds may seem trivial, but it's not. Even though in the moment students may not appear to care about the inquiry, they do. I recently taught a group of graduate students. Their program was rigorous and stressful. I began every class of the semester in the way that I just described. Here are just two of the comments that I received via the reflection papers that I assigned that speak directly to the positive impact of starting each class this way.

"Professor Bunn is the first teacher I ever had who showed a genuine interest in how my classmates and I are feeling. Before each lecture he would ask, 'How are you doing? How do you feel about the class so far?' I really appreciated that." Another comment was, "I liked that Professor Bunn began class by asking us how we are doing? It was nice to know someone cared about us. He's the only teacher in our program who asked us how we are feeling."

CHAPTER FORTY-SEVEN

A Teacher Is Never the Right Age

TEACHING IS THE ONLY job where a person's age is always a potential deficit. A new teacher is considered too young. The perception is that he/she does not have enough professional or life experience to be effective. Then when the teacher gets older, he/she is perceived to be "out of touch" with the current generation. A teacher can't win the age battle.

I talked about the exchange I had with a student my first day as a teacher when I was young. Now at age fifty, the eighteen-year-old students that I have in my classroom, from a chronological and a technological sense, move further and further away. If I make a reference to the band Pink Floyd, I get weird looks. When I mention that there were no computers in classrooms when I was in high school, students are shocked. When I explain that I don't do social media nor do I have a smart phone, students look genuinely concerned regarding my well-being, as if to say, "That's awful. How can you live that way?"

My advice is to embrace where you are. You have no choice. Don't try to be something you are not to identify with your students. They see right through this. Just be yourself. I frequently use the differences in how things were when I was growing up compared to how things are now as a clinical history lesson. It's educational. Students like a good story, and as an experienced therapist I have many of them. Compare and contrast the gap in your age and experience. And most importantly, do not judge them for being addicted to their smart phones or other generationally driven change. The world you grew up in is gone. This is their world. Show them empathy and help them learn how to navigate it.

CHAPTER FORTY-EIGHT

Forget Power Point Slides.
Do Power Lectures.

I THINK THE INVENTION of power point was extremely detrimental to the educational process. Why do I think that? Simple, the students have told me. Many teachers are content to stand in the corner of the room in front of a computer and read bullets to the students directly from slides. It has made the task of doing a lecture too easy. Presentations done in this manner bore the students and prevent them from connecting with the teachers in a meaningful way. It also decreases the amount of time that teachers need to prepare for class, and I would wager this is the main appeal to lecturing this way.

I teach primarily from memory. As a result of feedback that I once got from students letting me know it is difficult to take notes in my class in the absence of overhead notes, I began using the overhead. I now put a slide on the overhead that the students can refer to as I lecture so if something is missed, they can use the slide as a reference point. But the slides I use are for the students, not for me. I don't refer to them at all. And I certainly don't stand in the corner of the room and read from them. By memorizing my lectures, I can wander the room freely, make eye contact, speak with passion, and connect with the students.

One student wrote to me the following. "It's so nice to have a teacher that can stand in front of the room and lecture from memory. This shows that you care enough to spend time preparing for us and lends credibility to what you are saying." Another student wrote, "We can read power point slides on our own. We come to class to get a deeper understanding of the material. I like that you don't just stand there and read off slides like my other teachers do." Another comment read, "I am impressed that you deliver powerful lectures class after class from memory. That makes me as interested in the material as you are. I know that takes work. And knowing that you work so hard for this class made me want to work hard too." And one more comment read, "The way you lecture makes me feel like you are talking to me and not at me. Teachers who just stand there and read from slides can't hold my attention. I actually find myself paying even more attention in your class because I don't want to miss anything."

The students have spoken. All the above comments were made randomly by students I've taught over the years. It is important to note here that I have never directly asked students for their opinions regarding my lecture style. I consistently request feedback from students about my classes, but they are free to focus on whatever they want. It's interesting how many students over the years have chosen to specifically point out how they find power point-driven lectures to be boring and unable to hold their attention. One student even said, "It is impossible for me to get excited about class material that that the teacher is not excited about presenting. Teachers who just read from slides don't have any passion."

CHAPTER FORTY-NINE

Do the Assignments Too.

DURING THE SEMESTER, I give writing assignments that are geared towards self-reflection. They are purposeful and lend meaning to the class. Students consistently report enjoying these writing assignments better than doing the standard research paper on Jung or Freud because these assignments have meaning for them. These assignments help them experience personal growth and self-awareness.

As a teacher, I think it is important to lead via example. It is for this reason that I do the writing assignments too. I typically read an example of a gratitude letter that I have written to someone, out loud to the class to give them a sense of what I am looking for them to do when they write their letters. I openly discuss "awakening experiences" that I've had in my life to give them an idea of how to pick out such experiences they've had. I openly talk about my own destructive self-talk patterns and how they make me feel when I let them get the best of me. Students appreciate this kind of sharing. A student wrote to me in a final reflection paper, "In your class I felt comfortable sharing things about my life. And I really liked that you shared things about your life with us. It showed that you trusted us too and it wasn't one-sided."

CHAPTER FIFTY

Don't Teach a Class, Create an Experience

WHEN I WAS A student, I was in a class where we were doing presentations. At one point the teacher said something that I have always remembered. He said, "You are not convincing me. If it is not real to you, it is not real to me. If it means nothing to you, then it means nothing to me. Where is your passion?" Great question. I will pose the same one to you. Where is your passion? Do you have any?

Teachers who are passionate create a meaningful experience for their students. Passion cannot be fabricated. Either you feel strongly about what you are presenting, or you don't. Passion lends energy, excitement, and credibility to a presentation. When students learn from a teacher who presents the material in a passionate way, the teacher creates an experience. A student recently shared in a reflection paper, "I loved this *experience* and will hold it near to my heart." A class quickly fades from memory, but a meaningful experience will be remembered forever.

CHAPTER FIFTY-ONE

Make Direct Observations and Share Them

THROUGHOUT THIS BOOK I have discussed and referred to how I solicit for anonymous feedback from my students to get an accurate sense of their experiences in my class. It is important for me to know how students are feeling about my class. It is equally important for them to know how I am feeling. We are in a relationship and I owe it to them to share my observations with them appropriately when I feel the need to do so. The kind of observations I am discussing here are global and apply to the entire class. This is a simple yet powerful process that students appreciate. Doing this helps to facilitate the academic alliance and demonstrates that I care enough about them to share my feelings. The following is an example of a direct observation that I made to one of my classes a few years ago.

"I am getting a sense that we are not connecting now the way we did when the semester began. When I present questions to the group, I get little to no response, and quite honestly, most of you seem disinterested at this point. I feel like I have lost you somewhere along the way. I am going to ask for anonymous feedback today. Please let me know your respective thoughts about this. Is there something that needs to change?" Unfortunately, the feedback

I received was generic and not helpful. I got responses like, "The class is going fine. No complaints here." And, "I think everything is good so far. You don't need to change anything."

Every relationship has two responsible parties. This conversation did not generate a major change in the class. This was a group that lost momentum and it was never successfully reestablished. But even though the change I'd hoped for did not happen, two very important lessons were conveyed here. One, I showed the students how to appropriately express one's feelings when there is a problem. Second, I taught them a lesson in responsibility. I could have easily chosen to ignore the fact that we were experiencing a communication problem. But instead, I took responsibility for my feelings and chose to express them. The fact that nothing changed is not relevant. What is relevant is that I provided the students an opportunity to suggest things they would like me to change. Suggesting changes was their responsibility. And of course, I had to explore the possibility that their perspective and mine were simply different. My observation that there was a communication problem was just that, my observation. Perhaps I was bored with them and projected this feeling onto them.

CHAPTER FIFTY-TWO

The Students Are Innocent
Beware Countertransference

COUNTERTRANSFERENCE IS A CONCEPT that is typically examined in the context of a traditional therapeutic relationship between a therapist and a client. That phenomenon that takes place when the therapist begins having a strong emotional response to the client. This is the result of the client reminding the therapist of someone from the past, perhaps some unresolved issue that the therapist has yet to deal with.

In the classroom, the same kind of dynamic is possible. Despite any differences teachers and students have, one thing there is in common is that we all went to school. School was a great experience for some teachers, and perhaps not so great for others. What was your experience? Did you get bullied? Were you popular? Were you not popular but jealous of people who were? Were you an athlete? Did you fit in? Were you a great student? Were you the geek of the class? Did someone break your heart? These and many other questions should be examined and dealt with by teachers before they start teaching, lest they subconsciously mistreat some students and show favoritism towards others.

If you plan to teach for any length of time, you will see that time after time the same students find their way to you. They have similar looks, personalities, and interests as people you knew in your previous life, and that is where the danger lies. When I first started teaching, I only had the people I went to school with to compare these students to. Now I have been teaching long enough that students from my current classes not only remind me of people I went to school with, but of students I have taught over the years. This is very powerful.

Every semester the same female student shows up in one of my classes who reminds me of a girl who broke my heart in high school. The same male athlete strolls in who was popular and whom I envied so much for the treatment he got. And there is sometimes even a "clique" of three or four students who are joined at the hip and signed up for the class together. They walk into the room as a group that reminds me of groups like that when I was in school who thought they were better than everyone else. Then there is the student who reminds me of my best friend, and sometimes the student who reminds me of the first girl I ever kissed is there too.

And there it is. Semester after semester, the countertransference in action. But I am consciously aware of who these people are and who they remind me of. Are you? Have you even thought about it? As teachers, we run the risk of projecting our feelings, both positive and negative, onto our students. If we are not aware of these things, the negative feelings can cause us to be tougher on or less patient with a student who strongly reminds us of someone from the past whom we did not like. Also, our positive feelings from the past may motivate us to give special treatment and show favoritism towards students who remind us of someone whom we really cared about.

Neither scenario is appropriate, both scenarios are possible, and both must be avoided. It is my thinking that anyone who is going to become a teacher should be made to undergo at least one round of intensive psychotherapy to avoid this and many other potential problems. I like therapy, and I have participated in it for many years of my life. It is the only way to really raise awareness of what your "stuff" is, what your "issues" are, and how to keep it all in check.

We are all human. It's normal that when we see people who remind us of the past that various feelings emerge. It's not appropriate however to allow those feelings to impact our behavior and the way we treat our students. Remember, the student in front of you now, despite the similarities, is not the person who bullied you, broke your heart, or was your best friend. This student is innocent.

CHAPTER FIFTY-THREE

Share What You Have
Learned About Life

A STUDENT ONCE ASKED me, "What is the best thing about being a therapist?" I responded, "There are two things. One, helping people become better versions of themselves. And two, learning vicariously from the mistakes of other people." Working in the field of human services, one gets to witness first hand what most other people only read about in the paper or see on television. I frequently use examples from my work as a clinician and my years as a teacher to explain to students how certain decisions generate certain consequences. This is a brief but important lesson I wanted to share here. Experience lends itself to credibility. Use what you have learned throughout your career to teach your students valuable lessons about life. Those experiences illuminate the course material and make for very entertaining stories. Your students will appreciate both.

CHAPTER FIFTY-FOUR

The Journey Ends but the Impact Remains

IN A TRADITIONAL THERAPEUTIC relationship, the therapist will begin preparing a client in advance for when the relationship is going to end. And it will end. Because of the kind of relationship that I am typically able to establish with my students, I think a termination process is appropriate here as well.

Naturally as the semester is winding down, it is obvious the relationship will be ending soon because final exams are coming up, final projects are due, final papers must be handed in. It seems the word final is neatly woven in at this point in the semester as a constant reminder that the end is near. Since that is the case, why is a termination process necessary?

Well, for some it probably isn't. If no real connection is made between the teacher and the students, the ending of the semester probably won't matter all that much to anyone. However, if you choose to utilize the techniques and strategies that I have outlined in this book, and you do so effectively, the ending of the semester will generate some feelings. These feelings will be experienced by at least some of the students, and most definitely by you. Sometimes I think teachers hide behind barriers and refrain from letting the students really "matter" to them, because of how painful the termination process can be.

I think it's important to let our students matter to us. It's important too that we matter to them. The conversations I have with students, the way I present, the things I choose to share, and the writing assignments are all "content" oriented. The content of our conversations is what dictates how meaningful they will become. You probably remember the conversation you had with someone about the death of their loved one more than a discussion you had with someone about the weather or the score of the ball game. That is how it works. Expressing feelings, sharing experiences, and showing compassion lays the groundwork for a meaningful experience. And is it not sad when a meaningful experience draws to its natural conclusion?

Boundaries were not meant to be barriers, but some teachers hide behind them as if they were. Boundaries are meant to provide guidelines of safety to dictate what can be shared and with whom. Use your clinical judgment. Let that direct you. Not all students will respond to these techniques the same way. Like everything else, students will get out of it what they put into it. I've had my share of students who have earned an A, but who really didn't learn anything. I've also had students who earned a C but benefitted greatly from the life lessons and the relationship.

The final assignment that I sometimes give is simply called a "self-reflection" paper. This assignment is geared towards motivating students to really look at everything that has taken place between us during our semester together. I ask them to express how they feel about it. I like them to address the goals we set at the beginning of the semester. Did our work together help the student to become a better version of him/herself? Did I successfully create the academic alliance with them? I give these questions as a starting point, but the paper is a mechanism for their self-reflection so they can talk about anything they like.

Last semester when I gave this assignment, here are some comments that students included in their self-reflection papers. "I found myself becoming emotional during our last class together. I didn't realize the impact this class truly had on me until it was about to end." Another comment. "There were times this semester when things got tough, that your class was the only thing I had to look forward to. I wish it wasn't over." And finally, "Even though I didn't know what to expect from this class in the beginning, it quickly became my favorite class. I am going to miss it." When the content of class discussions and assignments is meaningful, a connection takes place and the class takes on an emotional component as well.

Throughout this book, the students whom it has been my privilege to teach have spoken to you. You have heard their voices through the feedback I have shared with you. Their comments are the natural result of establishing meaningful relationships enriched with content. Creating an experience that was worth their time and effort. Ultimately, facilitating their personal growth and successfully helping them to become better versions of themselves. To move closer to becoming the person they are meant to be, or rather, the person they choose to be.

My style of teaching takes a lot energy and a lot of planning. The way I do things demonstrates to my students that I have a definitive interest in their success. They know I care. I want them to look back on their time in my class and remember it as a meaningful experience that was a great use of their time. I do the very best that I can to make this happen. I hope you will too.

Bibliography

Corey, Gerald. *Theory and Practice of Counseling and Psychotherapy.* 10th ed. Boston: Cengage, 2017.

May, Rollo. *The Courage to Create.* New York: Norton, 1975.

Yalom, Irvin D. *Existential Psychotherapy.* New York: Basic, 1980.

———. *The Gift of Therapy: An Open Letter to a New Generation of Therapists and Their Patients.* New York: HarperCollins, 2002.

———. *Staring at the Sun: Overcoming the Terror of Death.* San Francisco: Jossey-Bass, 2009.

www.ingramcontent.com/pod-product-compliance
Lightning Source LLC
Chambersburg PA
CBHW070923270326
41927CB00011B/2696